Better Homes and Gardens®

small kitchen
solutions

WILEY

John Wiley & Sons,

P9-DBY-499

For general information about our other products and services, please contact our Customer Care Department within the United States at (800) 762-2974, outside the United States at (317) 572-3993 or fax (317) 572-4002.

Wiley also publishes its books in a variety of electronic formats. Some content that appears in print may not be available in electronic books. For more information about Wiley products, visit our web site at www.wiley.com.

ISBN 978-0-470-61294-1

Printed in the United States of America

10 9 8 7 6 5 4 3 2 1

Note to the Readers:
Due to differing conditions, tools, and individual skills, John Wiley & Sons, Inc., assumes no responsibility for any damages, injuries suffered, or losses incurred as a result of following the information published in this book. Before beginning any project, review the instructions carefully, and if any doubts or questions remain, consult local experts or authorities. Because codes and regulations vary greatly, you always should check with authorities to ensure that your project complies with all applicable local codes and regulations. Always read and observe all of the safety precautions provided by manufacturers of any tools, equipment, or supplies, and follow all accepted safety procedures.

welcome

Good things come in small packages. That often-heard missive applies to the 30 kitchens featured in this book. Simply put, *Better Homes and Gardens® Small Kitchen Solutions* celebrates smallness—and the clever approaches homeowners and designers have taken to shower their cooking spaces with style and function.

What constitutes a small kitchen? That depends on your vantage point. A small kitchen in a Midwestern home might seem like a cooking paradise in a New York City apartment, where one can often spread arms and touch walls on both sides. Our featured rooms run the gamut from pint-size to modestly sized. The commonality is that they've done a lot with a little. Let the photographs and stories inspire your own ideas for finagling a tight floor plan, stretching storage, and embracing style. The Kitchen Workbook section at the back of this book will help you narrow down choices in cabinets, countertops, and more. Whether you're in the dreaming or doing stage of remodeling, remember that dimensions are only numbers. Even in a small kitchen, the sky is the limit.

contents

1 Compact Creativity 6

Rekindled Charm 8

Presto Change-o 14

Sociably Sleek 20

Fancy Footprint 26

Simply Organized 30

Cozy with Color 36

Smooth Move 42

Little Wonder 46

2 Everyday Elegance 52

Worth the Wait 54

Vigorously Vintage 60

Sleek Chic 66

Details, Details 72

Warm Embrace 78

Glass Act 84

3 Open Horizons 90

Tailored for Today 92

Perfect Harmony 98

Nested Interest 104

City Cottage 108

Passing Through 114

Age Appropriate 120

4 Dream Rooms, Real Budgets 124

Overdue Update 126

Kitchen by the Sea 132

Bounce-Back Bungalow 138

Splash of Color 144

Buried Treasure 150

5 Culinary Delights 156

Small but Mighty 158

Deco Perfecto 162

Bright Spot 166

Maximized Modern 170

Taking Stock 174

6 Kitchen Workbook 178

Cabinets 180

Countertops 182

Backsplashes 184

Sinks and Faucets 185

Floors 186

Lighting 187

Resources 188

compact
creativity

1

Amazing things happen when you embrace the possibilities. Imagine soffits removed so new cabinets can stretch to the ceiling, making your kitchen seem grander. Consider how a short peninsula could substitute for the island you simply can't fit into the room. Think about how a built-in can bring function to an awkward nook, or how toe-kick drawers could eke out an extra bit of storage on base cabinets. The kitchens on the following pages incorporate those design-smart features and more. They're glass-half-full kinds of spaces.

Getting your kitchen to reach its full potential starts by looking beyond what it is to what it could be. List—and rank—your priorities. Then let those priorities guide your makeover and inspire clever ways to work them in. Remember, it's not the size of the room that matters, but what you do with it. Even in a small kitchen, you can do a lot.

White cabinetry, big windows, and skylights brighten this kitchen. A reproduction pendant gives the sink area period-inspired flair.

rekindled charm

Floor to ceiling, this kitchen brims with vintage style and space-stretching savvy.

Living in an old house usually means learning to compromise. In exchange for charm and character, the owners get small rooms and limited storage. Such was the case in this 1916 home—originally built as a one-room cabin—in Mill Valley, California. When architectural designer David Rivera signed on to remodel the kitchen, he knew that restoring the charm would be easy. The trickier part was how to make the small space seem larger and give it adequate storage without adding on.

For Rivera, the ceiling was an obvious starting point to mine space—or at least to visually mine it. Removing the low ceiling stretched the room upward. The new slanted ceiling that allowed Rivera to work in the extra height adds to the charm—or quirk—of the home. While the ceiling went up, a half-wall that hemmed in the work core came down, instantly making the kitchen seem larger.

New skylights, a wall of windows, and a glass door also help visually expand the room. "They bring the outside in," Rivera says. So, too, does a wide window over the sink. It looks out to a colorfully landscaped yard—a calming view that makes doing dishes seem less of a chore.

In keeping with the don't-close-it-in strategy, Rivera choose classic white cabinetry over stained cabinets. "The cabinet style is consistent with the cottage style of the house," he says. He also took inspiration from features common to old homes:

built-ins. Here, built-ins streamline the space and fill in a few awkward gaps. The microwave integrates into upper cabinetry near the refrigerator, freeing up countertop space. At the back of the kitchen, cabinets fill a nook. With glass doors and beaded-board backing, the cabinets resemble a china hutch and create a charming point of interest visible from the exterior door on the opposite wall.

Without doubt, the most prominent built-in is the cushioned bench that stretches along the exterior wall, making efficient use of space below all the windows. The bench is multifunctional: It provides sunny seating and also incorporates storage. The homeowners use it store their recyclables. Across from it, a built-in bookcase holds cookbooks and provides an out-of-the-cooking-zone counter for keys and mail.

ABOVE: Glass-front cabinets turn a narrow wall into a display space. "The glass doors extend the sight lines and make the kitchen appear larger," says architectural designer David Rivera. OPPOSITE: Rivera used vertical space to make the most of the cooking area. The stainless-steel backsplash above the range incorporates a shelf for warming plates or cooked foods. The range hood is outfitted with warming and task lights, as well as a high-powered exhaust system.

Because the kitchen isn't large, Rivera limited surfaces to just a few colors so as not to overwhelm the room. Surfaces are essentially black or white, creating a timeless scheme. Gray honed limestone countertops are a shade up from black to ensure they don't eat up the light.

Although the ceiling received the initial attention, it's the checkerboard floor that steals the show. Oversize black and white squares painted on the existing wood create a budget-friendly floor that's the room's eye-catcher. As one of the homeowners put it, "You can have a smaller, simple kitchen that still has a wow factor to it."

❝ The cabinet style is consistent with the cottage style of the house. ❞

—ARCHITECTURAL DESIGNER DAVID RIVERA

ABOVE: The slanted ceiling adds extra height. The built-in bookcase's open and closed storage allows flexibility in what can be stored in it. With cookbooks and mixing bowls, it serves as a mini baking center. RIGHT: The painted wood floor is the room's focal point. FAR RIGHT: For continuity, the storage bench has the same facing as the kitchen cabinets and the same curved feet as the bookcase. OPPOSITE LEFT: The sink is mounted under the countertop so crumbs can be wiped directly into it. The single bowl accommodates a bevy of dishes and large pots. OPPOSITE RIGHT: Curved edges created from two pieces of limestone dress up the countertops.

THIS PHOTO: An arched eating nook and door inspired the curved cabinetry in this cozy-looking kitchen.

presto change-o

As if by magic, a designer transforms a tired kitchen into a vintage charmer.

ABOVE: Space-stretching details include this display shelf above the backsplash. It's a perfect spot for coffee mugs.

Kitchen designer Cherie Brown, a member of the National Kitchen & Bath Association (NKBA), used a bag of tricks to update Shirley and Ken Dreyer's kitchen without changing the room's footprint.

It was like pulling a rabbit out of a hat. The small space—remodeled in the 1950s—had pink metal cabinets, poorly placed appliances, and obstacles such as a radiator, flue, and laundry chute. The couple had made it work, though, through two kids and 30 years. "Our house is like an old friend—we had really grown with it," Shirley says. "We wanted to keep it as it was, but make our old kitchen new."

Take-Home Tip
Curved cabinets improve the flow in a small kitchen by turning sharp, tight corners into smooth segues.

The radiator, flue, and laundry chute stayed—they're now better disguised—but the cabinets, appliances, and some sharp corners did a disappearing act. Inspired by arches in the 1920s Tudor-style home, Brown incorporated curves in the new cabinetry to boost openness and improve flow. "Anytime you extend a line with a curve or angle, it draws your eye and appears bigger," Brown says.

Another trick was using 15-inch-deep upper cabinets instead of standard 12-inch units, which increased storage by 25 percent. Handy shelves and drawers are worked in wherever possible, including the ends of curved cabinets. The microwave is an over-the-cooktop model, and the dishwasher is only 18 inches wide. "When you don't have an endless supply of space, you work with everything you have," Brown says. "Most people don't have any idea all the little things that can make a kitchen work harder."

Her audience is delighted. "We think we improved the way the kitchen fits in with the rest of the house, and we had so much fun doing it," Ken says. "Cherie knew how much our hearts were in it."

ABOVE: A narrow pullout on the left side of the sink and an 18-inch-wide dishwasher on the right (disguised as a set of drawers) save space. Curved cutouts in the cabinet doors play off the arches in the room. RIGHT: Using soapstone for the backsplash, countertops, and sink creates a continuous block of color that makes the area seem deeper and wider. OPPOSITE: Oak benches with leather upholstery upgraded an existing eating nook. The table features a marble top and wrought-iron base. It's a visually light alternative to a bulky wood table typically found in an old eating nook.

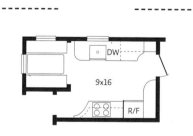

EFFICIENT FLOW
Rounding the ends of cabinet sections created a greater sense of openness while maintaining the efficiency of the existing galley-style layout. Windows and doorways connect the kitchen to other rooms and to the outdoors.

sociably sleek

No space goes to waste when a designer turns an unfriendly U-shape kitchen into an engaging contemporary room that suits a couple to a T.

The kitchen is a top social networking site. It's like Facebook for your home, a place for connecting with family and friends—only it's done in person. But if the space isn't well-planned, connections are difficult to make, says Richard Landon, a certified master kitchen and bath designer (CMKBD) and member of the National Kitchen & Bath Association (NKBA).

"The U-shape kitchen with the cooktop on one leg—the most despised kitchen plan ever conceived—isolates the cook," Landon says. "There is no way to have interaction with someone not standing right next to you."

Landon says the typical U-shape layout includes a bank of upper cabinets hung above a breakfast bar that nobody uses. "If you walk into almost any remodeled 1990s kitchen, you'll see that scar tissue in the ceiling where those upper cabinets have been ripped away," he says.

Malei and Robert Davidson had such a U-shape arrangement in their Seattle kitchen. "The wall cabinets did block me from guests, and I really wanted to have an island to work on instead of the peninsula," Malei says. They hired Landon to transform the room.

Boosting base cabinets and minimizing upper units made this kitchen feel more open without losing storage. The eating bar features pneumatic stools.

ABOVE: **For a contemporary look, designer Richard Landon mixed white base cabinets, zebrawood uppers, and lift-up units that feature doors of stainless steel and reeded glass. A corner appliance garage capitalizes on a cache of space.** ABOVE RIGHT: **Narrow pullout spice racks on the appliance wall show Landon's penchant for using every sliver of space.** OPPOSITE: **The corner cooktop, set in a stainless-steel countertop, basks in the light of enlarged windows. The deep cabinets and countertop allow extra storage and work space, plus the extra distance from the windows accommodates a ceiling-mount hood.**

The couple's goal was a kitchen that could be a hot spot for social gatherings and also user-friendly when it's just the two of them. Initially Malei thought it would be impossible to get everything they wanted. "The kitchen was so small, I didn't see how we could ever have the room," she says. "Richard, though—well, he can find space anywhere."

Landon made room for an island by creating a wall of appliances, including stacked ovens and a built-in refrigerator, that pushes the backs of the units into the adjacent dining room. There, the appliances are camouflaged by shallow display cabinets painted white to match existing trimwork. Glass doors make the unit look like a china hutch.

Landon also found a way to remove the view-blocking hanging cabinets without losing storage capacity. He made the new base cabinets taller than normal, which boosted their storage volume and raised the height of the countertops. That was a relief

Take-Home Tip
Remember that sinks come in all sizes. Squeeze a small sink in by the cooktop to fill pots and rinse foods.

to 6-foot-2 Robert, who got a sore back from hunching over standard 36-inch-high countertops. "These counters are 38 inches high," Landon says. "In fact, it's rare that I do standard counters here in the Northwest. We are the tallest people in the country, really."

The designer's cleverness didn't end there. The extra-tall base cabinets include a row of drawers built into the toe-kicks. "It's like an additional top drawer," Landon says. The cabinets and drawers are extra-deep, too. "I rarely do standard depths of 24 inches," Landon says. "These are 30 inches deep, and you get a tremendous increase in capacity with that."

Minimizing upper cabinets made the kitchen more welcoming, Landon says. "It transitions easily into the family room, and it feels very much like a hug when you step into it."

The space also feels much brighter, thanks to another Landon trick—bumping up the heights of the windows on the sink wall. "With a two-story home you can get substantially more light if you move the header above the window up into the rim joist of the second floor," he says. And the extra 6 inches per window makes a big difference. "To me, the old space was like it was half asleep, its eyes were half closed," Landon says. "Now, you can see the sky."

kitchen looks good as it works well and uses space efficiently.

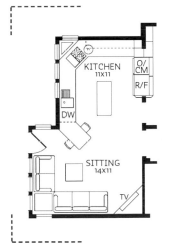

UPDATING THE U

An obsolete U-shape layout with a peninsula was tweaked to add an island and make the kitchen more open to a sitting area. The main sink, corner cooktop, and angled eating counter occupy an exterior wall, where they benefit from windows, while the refrigerator and ovens are on an interior wall.

ABOVE LEFT: Raising the base cabinets and countertop a few inches created room for toe-kick drawers faced in stainless steel. ABOVE: To make room for the island, Landon pushed the backs of the refrigerator and ovens into the dining room, then disguised them with shallow storage units resembling china cabinets. OPPOSITE LEFT: The main sink, which includes a recessed drying rack, is integrated into the stainless-steel countertop for a clean look. The backsplash is back-painted reeded glass. OPPOSITE RIGHT: Landon adorned the island with custom pulls and stiletto heel legs. The countertop is an enameled lava stone that's virtually indestructible, while the zebrawood base boasts trimwork of wenge and walnut.

KITCHEN 11X11 / O/CM / R/F / DW / SITTING 14X11 / TV

Daring dark
cabinets and
stainless-steel
appliances make
a once-blah
kitchen sleek and
sophisticated.

fancy footprint

Finding a place for everything and putting everything in its place: that was the strategy for making this kitchen livable. The room's rich, sophisticated look was the bonus.

before

ABOVE: **The sink and appliances occupy the same places as before, but the new models are more functional and fashionable. The restaurant-style faucet serves a serious cook.** OPPOSITE TOP, LEFT: **Kitchen designer Candice Dickinson paired dark-stained cabinets with quartz-surfacing countertops that contain olive-color flecks.** OPPOSITE TOP, RIGHT: **Stacking the washer and dryer let Dickinson shrink a laundry room and fold the extra space into the kitchen.** OPPOSITE BOTTOM: **A portion of the old laundry room became the bar, which connects the kitchen to the dining and living areas.**

"Well-designed storage is critical and every cabinet must have a purpose," says Candice Dickinson, a certified kitchen designer (CKD) and member of the National Kitchen & Bath Association (NKBA). "You have to make every inch count."

Located in a house that has just under 900 square feet, the old kitchen had the same compact footprint as the newly remodeled version, but lacked light and pizzazz. "There were boring white oak cabinets, laminate countertops, and just two small windows," Dickinson says. "And the laundry room had side-by-side units housed behind four bifold doors that took up way too much of the limited square footage."

Although Dickinson kept the same basic layout and appliance placements, she transformed the room by cutting the space-hogging laundry room in half (the washer and dryer are now stacked) and turning the extra square footage into a bar that links the kitchen to living and dining areas. She set back the bar cabinetry and countertop a bit to make room for a table and chairs. "The change made the space feel much bigger because I was able

to open up part of the kitchen to the living room," Dickinson says. "Before, all you could see from the living area was a big blank wall, and now you see into the kitchen."

The bar area is a model of efficiency, offering handy wine cubbies, a surface for beverage prep that doubles as food-serving space for buffets, undercounter storage, and glass-front cabinets for stemware. "I even managed to tuck in an extra cabinet behind the glassware," Dickinson says.

Replacing a window by the dining area with French doors went a long way toward brightening the once-dreary room—plus, the doors provide access to a patio and grill. Eliminating a soffit that stretched around the perimeter of the room added vertical space and allowed Dickinson to extend upper cabinets to the ceiling. And lengthening the range wall by several inches at one end created more counter space, making the cooking area feel less cramped. "I was also able to get equal-size drawers on either side of the stove and create better storage as a result," Dickinson says.

The homeowner's dark-wood dining table inspired the kitchen's ebony-stained cabinets, which Dickinson paired with olive-flecked quartz-surfacing countertops. The dark wood was a bold design move in a modest-size space. "Even though the kitchen is small, I wasn't afraid to introduce dark cabinets, because I thought the contrast with the stainless-steel appliances and cross-reeded glass on the laundry door would be striking and sophisticated," she says.

It's an old design trick: Add glass fronts to cabinetry. The perception of greater depth increases the visual space of this kitchen.

before

simply organized

Creativity trumps limitations in this makeover. The kitchen is now tidy and functional—yet still very small.

You'd think that after traipsing through a gazillion houses as a kitchen and home scout for Better Homes and Gardens®, Betsy Harris would have the crème de la crème of kitchens. Why, then, did it take this accomplished cook almost 20 years to finally remodel her own kitchen?

The first reason is one that any homeowner who has spent months walking the aisles of home centers and flipping through magazines can understand: saturation. "I am exposed to so many new and exciting ideas and products that in some ways, it can be difficult to make decisions about my own kitchen," Betsy says.

For years Betsy would come home after a photo shoot and see right past the 35-year-old range, circa-1940 sink, fake wood laminate countertops, and dark blue cabinets painted to match the car siding backsplash, a tongue-and-groove paneling that was all the rage back in the early 20th century.

"It was such a challenge to prepare food—I hand-washed all the dishes because I didn't have a dishwasher—but I was basically content with the kitchen's quirkiness," she says. "And the small size, at roughly 9×8 feet, puts everything at my fingertips."

When two coils on her stove top stopped working, Betsy began warming to the thought of a makeover. That notion heated up when her oven went on the blink. Soon, the idea caught fire and she and her husband, Art, were collecting paint swatches and comparing the merits of more counter space versus a standard-size refrigerator.

Betsy had a few parameters. Because her house was a historical log cabin, she was stuck with the original footprint of

> **" Focus on the small details. They'll make a big difference in how your kitchen looks and works."**
>
> —HOMEOWNER BETSY HARRIS

LEFT: A countertop cabinet that's a twist on an appliance garage keeps small appliances handy and out of sight when they're not being used. OPPOSITE: Open shelving gives homeowner Betsy Harris the chance to change the look of her kitchen at will. She chose white dishes for their practicality and the way they blend with the color scheme. Colorful pieces would catch the eye and detract from the kitchen's serene feel.

the kitchen. Art insisted on keeping the car siding backsplash, beaded-board ceiling, and pine flooring. Everything else, the couple reasoned, could go—and did go.

Relying on her expertise, Betsy was adamant that "every inch of space be utilized and accounted for." She maximized storage space with upper and lower cabinetry, an appliance garage, undercounter refrigerator drawers, and pullouts wherever they would fit. "I gave up counter space for the appliance garage, but hiding the appliances behind doors contributes to the kitchen's clean, uncluttered look," Betsy says. "I also love the slide-out storage cabinet to the left of the range. It's only 9 inches wide, but it stores three levels of canned goods and bottles, keeping me from rooting around in the back of a cabinet. Plus, I don't know what else you could have done with that small of a space."

Betsy outfitted the kitchen with materials that had managed to stay on her list of perennial favorites. "I liked the clean look of white, Shaker-style cabinetry, and I wanted a few glass doors so I could display things," she says. Her other must-haves included

Pro Pointers

Homeowner and kitchen and home pro Betsy Harris has seen her share of design fiascoes. Her advice?

KNOW YOURSELF Consider not only your style preferences, but also how you cook and entertain. Though the trend over the past few years has been large, open kitchens, Betsy likes her small, intimate kitchen because of its convenience.

CHOOSE A DESIGN Find a look that fits with your home's architecture. Otherwise, the kitchen will look out of sync.

FOCUS ON SMALL DETAILS They can make a big difference. Cabinet hardware, lighting, windows, and accessories all contribute to your kitchen's style.

INVEST IN THE BEST Shop for the best quality cabinetry, countertops, and appliances that your budget will allow.

WORK WITH A PRO A professional can help you understand and clarify your wants and needs—and often save you money.

stainless-steel hardware, fixtures, and appliances—including a dishwasher. Betsy was always conscious of her budget, but she was willing to put money toward items that she knew would hold their value. "My biggest splurge was the honed black granite counters—pricey but classic," she says.

Although attracted to the classic "new country look," Betsy was fastidious in integrating the kitchen's design with her home's existing architecture. She restored the pine floors to their original golden tone, a nod to an earlier era. She painted the wood walls and backsplash a warm, faint gray, a hue that reads white without creating too stark a background.

Keeping the car siding and working with the existing footprint also added to the kitchen's charm. "In hindsight, I'm so glad Art insisted on keeping the wood ceiling, walls, and backsplash," Betsy says. "They are the key to making our more contemporary cabinetry and appliances look right in our antique home."

As an afterthought, Betsy added open shelving above the appliance garage, a design element that gives the eye a rest as it moves about the room. "I was an art major, and arranging items on those shelves gives me the same feeling as creating a still life," she says. "I also feel like a professional when I'm cooking because I can slide the plates right off the shelves, just like a chef does."

With the remodel complete, Betsy says the kitchen lives larger than ever and gives her everything she needs. "Friends can't believe it's a new kitchen in the same small space," she says. Now, when she's out hunting down the latest in kitchen style and design, Betsy no longer looks for the perfect kitchen—she knows she's already found it.

OPPOSITE TOP, LEFT: A pullout pantry adds accessibility to every inch of space—great by the range OPPOSITE TOP, RIGHT: A sliding tray ensures that there's no digging for pots and pans at the back of a cabinet. OPPOSITE BOTTOM, LEFT: The tall curved faucet is handy for cleaning oversize pots and pans. OPPOSITE BOTTOM, RIGHT: Sliding, stacked trays maximize storage and keep flatware organized.

1. LANDING STRIP
Because space was tight, the sink was placed adjacent to the range. There is landing space for cookware to the left of the range and a sliver of space on the right.

2. MAXIMIZE SPACE
A countertop cabinet maximizes space and keeps small appliances accessible.

3. NEW DISHWASHER
Space for a dishwasher was added to the new plan.

4. REFRIGERATOR DRAWERS
Refrigerator drawers were a splurge that the homeowners say are worth the expense.

cozy with color

After buying the 1920s home her grandparents built, this designer filled the kitchen with happy hues.

"My grandmother called it her dollhouse," says interior designer Kristi Dinner of the small Denver home that her grandparents built in 1928 and Kristi purchased for herself in 2001. "My mother was thrilled that I bought it, and I was delighted to have this rare chance to do whatever I wanted without having to bow to a client."

Budget constraints precluded any immediate large-scale remodeling, but the kitchen's nondescript white cabinets and laminate counters with oak edging—the results of a previous remodel—gnawed at Kristi's design sensibilities. When the time was right, she ripped everything out and started over.

"As far as the floor plan, there wasn't much we could do—the space was what it was," Kristi says. Architect Dean Lindsey helped her pinpoint an existing blank wall as the location for a floor-to-ceiling display cabinet to hold china, pottery, and glassware. "We replaced the shallow cabinets on the opposite wall with a curved breakfast bar that took up less space than what was there before," Lindsey says. "As a result, we could add the wall unit and still have room for a passageway."

Kristi bought new stainless-steel appliances, including a built-in steam oven and a glass-door refrigerator. She "floated" glass shelves near the new sink, which is an integral marble basin. "I like the continuous sweep of the veins," she says. The materials palette includes carrara marble countertops and apple-green and white backsplash tiles in basket-weave and river-stone patterns. "It was a lot of pattern," Kristi says, "but I figured if I couldn't take some risks in my own kitchen, where could I take them?"

Everything fell neatly into place except for the cabinetry. "I really struggled to find the perfect wood, but nothing seemed right," Kristi says. "Then I remembered a picture of a kitchen with

Bright colors and stainless steel power the new look of interior designer Kristi Dinner's kitchen. To save space, a shallow eating counter wraps around the walls of a stairwell.

red lacquer cabinets I'd cut out of a magazine years before, and I knew that was what I wanted."

The challenge was keeping the red and green from looking like Christmas. "It was the tone of green that ultimately made it all come together," says Kristi, who designed window treatments in the same hue. She also incorporated a Greek key element into the cabinetry design. "It's layered on the red doors, but on the wall unit I did more of a cutout because of the glass," she adds. "I like the way the key ties the kitchen together."

ABOVE: Like the countertops, the integral sink is carrara marble, a stone that conveys the vintage elegance of the home's 1920s roots. ABOVE RIGHT: The basket-weave backsplash pattern supplies contemporary energy. RIGHT: A Greek key design on one of the cabinet doors blends a classic pattern with modern color. Porcelain knobs resemble white tiles. OPPOSITE: The glass-front refrigerator breaks up the solidness of the bank of pantry cabinets.

SMALL COMFORT

The curved eating counter by the stairs is shallow enough to leave clearance between the stools and a new display unit on the opposite wall. A narrow, L-shape work core offers step-saving galley efficiency.

ABOVE LEFT: The center portion of the display cabinet is a lighted niche that incorporates a glass shelf and tiles in a river-stone pattern. ABOVE: Tapering the eating bar on the opposite wall let Kristi add this display cabinet and provide adequate clearance between the two. LEFT: Jewel-like pendants over the eating counter add 1920s glamour. OPPOSITE: The kitchen's footprint didn't change. This doorway still leads to the formal dining room, where Kristi continued the use of rich colors. Instead of refinishing the existing hardwood flooring, she painted it a dramatic black, adding another bold hue to the mix.

A widened doorway stretches this kitchen into the butler's pantry. To-the-ceiling cabinets accentuate the room's height and provide storage for items that aren't often used.

smooth move

This kitchen rises (and curves) to the challenge of restoring order and character.

The uncluttered layout and crisp, clean look of Andrew Wittman's San Francisco kitchen would inspire any cook. The old space—with aged appliances, chipped cabinets, and peeling laminate countertops—conspired against a chef. "It was an eyesore that never really felt clean," Andrew says of the 1950s version.

A disjointed layout with too many doorways and a lack of storage and work space meant that the kitchen functioned poorly for Andrew, who likes to cook and entertain. Interior designer Teneke Triggs and remodeler Paul Hines, both members of the National Kitchen & Bath Association (NKBA), collaborated to improve the room's function and flow while preserving the 1914 home's historical character.

Though other rooms retain their original dark-stained woodwork, Triggs knew that such a look would overwhelm the kitchen. So she and Andrew chose Edwardian-style cabinets in light gray and blue-gray, colors that echo softly in carrara marble countertops and tile.

Unexpected color and cabinets were only part of the solution. Triggs dealt with the poor layout by reconfiguring the space and shifting appliance positions. To make better use of space, she walled off one doorway to create an alcove for the built-in refrigerator, then moved the range to set off the professional-grade model. The sink is in the same spot—beneath large windows—but Triggs made the

sink cabinet a few inches deeper than is standard to allow more room for the faucets.

She also stretched the kitchen—and storage—by capitalizing on bonus space: a butler's pantry. After widening the doorway, she wrapped an L-shape cabinetry section around the jog between the two rooms. A rounded countertop and curved base cabinet turn the sharp corner into a smooth segue. Triggs gave one end of the sink-wall cabinetry the same rounded treatment. "I wanted to make the area between the kitchen and the butler's pantry as open as possible, and the best way to do that and still have storage was to make it rounded on both sides," she says.

While there's now a seamless transition between the two spaces, the added storage satisfies Andrew's desire for a highly organized and tidy kitchen. "I hate clutter, so places where appliances, utensils, and other items can be put away or lifted off the countertop were important," he says.

The tasteful mix of Edwardian elegance and modern-mindedness is appetizing for the cook and guests alike. "It's an attractive space that is very functional and practical," Andrew says. "It's just a delightful space to be in."

RIGHT: Base cabinets set on legs give the kitchen visual breathing room. OPPOSITE TOP: Marble countertops and backsplash tile bridge the contrasting cabinet colors. OPPOSITE BOTTOM, LEFT: In addition to its ceiling-height cabinets, this kitchen claims vertical space in small ways. On the backsplash, a rail system with shelves is a simple way to keep countertops clear so there's more available work space. OPPOSITE BOTTOM, MIDDLE: To allow room for the fixtures, the sink cabinet and countertop are a few inches deeper than normal. OPPOSITE BOTTOM, RIGHT: In the butler's pantry, glass shelves are a delicate alternative to a cabinet. With a wine refrigerator in the lower cabinet, the area is a handy bar.

TEAM PLAYERS
Widening a doorway helped the kitchen and butler's pantry read as one larger room. Curved cabinetry allows a seamless flow between the two spaces. The sink cabinet and countertop are rounded for visual softness and to ease traffic flow.

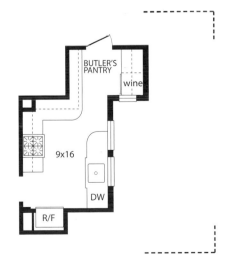

A prep peninsula plays the role of an island in this super-functional kitchen. The rounded end eases traffic flow.

little wonder

What's to love about this kitchen? Lots! It's packed with clever storage and the luxuries of a much bigger space.

You probably wouldn't expect Mark Gibson and Joe Terteling's 1925 bungalow on Seattle's Capitol Hill to echo with excess volume—no ballroom bedrooms or Queen Mary-size cooking quarters here. But come on. The existing kitchen was ridiculously small. Mark called it a "one-butt" kitchen, meaning that two people cooking at the same time was simply one derriere too many. "It was impossible," Joe says.

For a couple who love to cook, the crimp in their culinary creativity was almost tragic. Yet for nine years they endured. "The lot was too small for a bump-out, and there were design issues we just couldn't figure out," Joe says.

By the time they met up with designer Brian Parker, they had learned to love their home's character and simply wanted a little breathing room in the kitchen. What they got, however, was an ingenious rethinking of the floor plan and an offbeat design approach that was right-on.

The remodel didn't add an inch of square footage, but the kitchen lives much larger now. Parker found several areas where more storage could be squeezed into cabinets and walls. He ripped down a clunky, stacked-shelf pantry and replaced it with a pullout "food file" that has a recycling bin tucked underneath. He inserted two freezer drawers into an unused cabinet interior and turned a space-wasting coat closet into a slender envelope for slippers, boots, rain gear, and jackets. "The weather here is so wet and gunky that you have to have a place to keep slippers

by the door," Joe says. "Otherwise, there would be dirt and mud tracked all over the place."

Parker talked the pair down from their desire for an island. Plan revision after plan revision fell apart every time they inserted any kind of island. Finally, Parker proposed a peninsula with a prep sink on the end and access from both sides. "Think of it as an attached island," Parker told the couple. Eureka. "We can work together now," Joe says. "One at the prep sink, one making an entrée. Guests, too. We just put a bottle of wine on the peninsula and everyone wants to help."

With space issues settled, Joe and Mark focused on 1920s style. "We wanted a kitchen that matched the era," Joe says. "We had seen all the bells and whistles that you see on house tours, but we didn't want the industrial-commercial look that came with it. It would not have been right in a house with custom woodwork and leaded-glass windows." Interior designer Carleen Cafferty shared the couple's authenticity ethic. "I love everything to look like it was original, as much as possible," Cafferty says.

Accordingly, a hutch made to look like an original built-in anchors a small eating area, white subway tile covers the backsplash, and gray-green granite counters—honed to a matte finish—pick up the minty green of the range. "We spent half of the time trying to meld what would be historically accurate with what would be better functionally," Joe says. "Our goal was not to compromise the integrity for convenience or trends. So we don't have a coffee bar and espresso machine. I'd rather have a percolator, anyway."

TOP LEFT: Between doors to the dining room and powder room, a built-in hides the refrigerator and a narrow coat closet. TOP RIGHT: An apron-front sink conveys vintage style, as do double-hung windows with leaded-glass upper sashes. ABOVE: In the eating area, a banquette gave way to a more period-apt hutch. To the right are the pantry and basement door. OPPOSITE: A mint-green range cues a color scheme that recalls 1920s Coke bottles. Granite counters and linoleum flooring pick up the cue.

FAR LEFT: **In a small room, grab storage space wherever you can, even under the prep sink. The curved end of the peninsula opens, providing a spot for cleaning supplies and a compost pail.** LEFT: **Next to the back door—the entry from the garage—this built-in catches mail, messages, keys, and more. The fold-down bench is handy for someone putting on or taking off shoes.** MIDDLE ROW, FAR LEFT: **A pullout under the pantry and next to the basement door has bins for recyclables. Items can be kept here until it's time for curbside pickup.** MIDDLE ROW, LEFT: **One side of the built-in that holds the refrigerator is a slim coat closet with pullout shelves for shoes. The beefy handles are designed for exterior doors.** BOTTOM ROW, FAR LEFT: **Storage in the eating area includes a niche for a vintage rotary-dial phone that works—and rings loudly.** BOTTOM ROW, LEFT: **Two freezer drawers in the peninsula equip this spot to be a dessert bar or an extra prep station. A cutting board in the slot to the right pulls out from either side of the peninsula.**

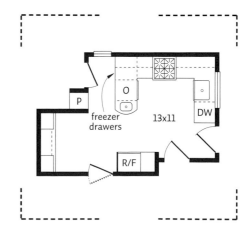

freezer drawers   13x11

P   O   DW   R/F

Handy Pantry

Joe Terteling and Mark Gibson found the idea for their "food file" in a magazine. The pullout pantry works like a filing cabinet, with each shelf holding a different food category. The shelves are labeled so that helpers can follow the system. "It's like the card catalog at the Library of Congress," Joe jokes.

The pantry keeps everything visible. "They can see right away what they're out of and need to restock," designer Brian Parker says. "In the old pantry, which was just a series of shelves in a closet, if you put something small behind something big, you'd lose it." Each shelf is about 18×21 inches. An extra-sturdy, German-made gliding mechanism handles the weight of bulk items and canned goods—up to 300 pounds.

More Storage Solutions
Consider these pantry storage ideas from other kitchens.

Many pantries are closed-door affairs, but this one is as open as can be for quick visual inventory. The shallow shelves save space—and there's a handy larder ladder.

A pantry can be a built-in or more like a freestanding furniture piece, such as this example. The white-painted, glass-panel doors with curtains elegantly enclose supplies.

The armoire-style design is popular for pantries. This one has shelves on the doors and deeper ones inside. Etched copper panels make the doors distinctive.

everyday elegance

2

As kitchens have become the heart of the home, it's only natural that they've become more stylish. Today, it's common to see cabinetry gracefully detailed with carved columns or curved brackets and exquisite tile backsplashes that are works of art. Kitchens are also showing their softer side, with pretty fabrics turned into window coverings, cushions, and even pillows that are tossed onto a bench.

But good looks aren't the end-all. After all, a kitchen still has to perform. When planning your space, look at the big picture and consider all the options to make sure you're not swayed by looks alone. A gorgeous countertop that needs frequent sealing may not suit your fuss-free lifestyle. If storage space is scarce, you may want to rethink clear glass cabinet doors; frosted glass gives a similar look without putting contents on display. As the following kitchens show, it is possible to have it both ways—pretty and practical.

worth the wait

Classic details ensure that a long-overdue update has lasting appeal.

LEFT AND ABOVE: The perimeter of this remodeled kitchen is awash in white. Keeping cabinetry, countertops, and the tile backsplash all the same color streamlines the room.

It took more than a decade for interior designer Agnes Hannah Friel to transform the dated kitchen of her most difficult client. That kitchen was her own, and she was the client. "I would get an idea, work on it, then put it away," Agnes Hannah says. "I kept putting it off because I couldn't get it just right."

The biggest roadblock was the room's modest size. Not wanting to add on to her 1940s Indianapolis home, Agnes Hannah kept searching for a way to make the 12×11-foot kitchen seem larger and function better, including squeezing in a place to eat. Finally concluding that she needed a fresh perspective, Agnes Hannah enlisted kitchen designer Kristin Zwitt. "Personally I think that smaller kitchens are more functional than larger ones," Zwitt says. "I hear homeowners say they need a bigger kitchen because they need more counter space. Why? Do they really have 304 different tasks going on at once?"

In no time, Zwitt made the room's size issues seem to vanish, starting by removing soffits above the old cabinets. "We couldn't make the room larger, but by removing the soffits we made it seem taller and bigger," Zwitt says. The new cabinets that stretch to the ceiling maximize storage; glass fronts on some cabinet doors visually open the room.

The trickiest part of the renovation was how to work in the eating space that topped Agnes Hannah's list. A traditional table wouldn't work in a snug layout, so Zwitt answered the call for dining with a short peninsula that juts from cabinets. "It's the star of the

LEFT: A metal rack that can withstand heat provides out-in-the-open storage above the cooktop. OPPOSITE LEFT: A foot pedal incorporated into the base of the sink cabinet activates the faucet. "When you have icky stuff on your hands, it's handy to be able to turn on the faucet with your foot," says homeowner and designer Agnes Hannah Friel. Above the double oven, a tall cabinet for less-used items maximizes storage. OPPOSITE RIGHT: A petite chandelier establishes the peninsula as a focal point and is a graceful touch in a hardworking kitchen.

room," Agnes Hannah says. Although the peninsula cuts into the walkway, which Zwitt prefers to avoid, its functionality outweighs the few extra steps around it.

Zwitt also worked wonders on the room's cooking functionality. She moved a doorway nine inches to allow for a double oven and grouped appliances and the sink into a tight but efficient work triangle. Agnes Hannah decided against facing appliances to blend them with the cabinetry. "I wanted my kitchen to look like a kitchen," she says.

That's not to imply the room is all business. Its elegance shows in the details, including carved columns and crown molding on cabinets. Black and white countertops set up a classic color scheme that repeats in the toile Roman shades on the window above the sink. "It allows me to bring in other colors and change things up," Agnes Hannah says.

The long-awaited renovation also inspired Agnes Hannah to change up her routine. She cooks a lot more now and savors time in her kitchen. She credits that shift to Zwitt's masterful design. "In a small room, it behooves you to use a kitchen professional to get a good plan and maximize your space," Agnes Hannah says. "What we were able to accomplish with the amount of space available exceeded my expectations."

ABOVE LEFT: Graceful curves transform vintage-inspired faucets into artful accessories. The small faucet is for drinking water. ABOVE: A pullout towel rack makes efficient use of a sliver of space between the dishwasher drawers and a corner cabinet. OPPOSITE: Columns flanking the sink cabinet add architectural interest.

vigorously vintage

Designer know-how conquers a charm deficiency to bring good looks and efficiency to this kitchen.

Graced with its original crown molding, built-ins, and hardwood floors, Janice and Dan Harrison's 1945 cottage-style home exuded all the warmth and character that the couple love about vintage homes. Unfortunately, all the charm stopped at the kitchen door. Floral wallpaper, faux-wood laminate countertops, and a pink tile floor had long outworn their welcome. To make matters worse, the kitchen consisted of little more than one wall of cabinetry and countertops—dismally inadequate storage and work space.

"Even though I hated it, I was still willing to ignore the kitchen's faults," Janice says. "But what really sent me over the edge was when the cupboards wouldn't close anymore because they had so much paint on them as a result of us repainting them over the years."

Janice sought the help of kitchen designers Marina Phillips and Dario Kiper, both members of the National Kitchen & Bath Association (NKBA). The duo took their style cues from the home. "We really wanted the kitchen to blend in with the house and look like it had always been there," Janice says.

Phillips carried the creamy colors of surrounding rooms into the kitchen with cabinetry painted a soft linen hue. Mission-style glass-front doors dress up cabinets and echo an original built-in glass display cabinet in the dining room. The cabinets showcase Janice's vintage glassware. Even the door to the garage is a step above the ordinary. It's outfitted with leaded

A new island-based layout makes Janice and Dan Harrison's kitchen work better, while its classic look suits their 1940s home.

glass, turning a usually overlooked feature into a showy focal point.

Black granite countertops and dark ceramic-tile flooring add dramatic counterpoints to the creamy tones. Other elements—vintage-look wavy glass, subway tile, bin-style door pulls, and beaded-board panels—stay true to the home's character.

Good-looking surfaces and thoughtful details, though, didn't interfere with functionality. "Janice was desperate for storage," Phillips says. "She was using a built-in ironing board cupboard to store her spices."

The floor plan complicated the quest for more storage. "There was an opening or window on every wall, which made it difficult to create flow and uninterrupted counter space," Phillips says. "We didn't want to make major structural changes, so adding

ABOVE LEFT: The simple backsplash visually bridges creamy cabinetry and green-flecked black-granite countertops. ABOVE: Janice likes to wash dishes by hand, so she wanted a deep single-basin sink for large pots and platters. OPPOSITE: With its eating counter and beaded-board paneling, the island offers function and charm.

> ## " We really wanted it to blend in with the house and look like it had always been there. "
>
> —HOMEOWNER JANICE HARRISON

on wasn't an option." Enlarging the openings to the dining room and family room left even less wall space.

Unfazed by the limitations, the design duo devised an efficient layout that doubled the amount of storage and counter space without expanding the footprint. Removing a corner eating area created space for a new island. Janice didn't want to lose the eat-in option entirely, so the island includes an overhang for two stools—a cozy setup for informal dining.

A new pantry and wine area flank the widened entry to the dining room, both boosting storage. The wine rack's slanted shelves inject modern flair into the space and add to the room's elegance.

Janice was so elated with the result that she hosted a holiday party shortly after the project was done. "Everyone ended up in the kitchen," she says. "People were there until two in the morning, so I guess you could say the kitchen was a big hit."

OPEN WIDE
Widening interior doorways opened this kitchen to adjoining rooms, but cut into storage. To make the most of the space that remained, one corner became a bar with a wine refrigerator. The other corner houses a built-in pantry.

ABOVE: A tall, storage-rich pantry stands beside a dressy door to the garage. OPPOSITE: Diagonal shelves for wine bottles, wavy glass, and crown molding detail the bar cabinetry.

A modest budget led to creative touches in this clean-lined kitchen. The backsplash is washable vinyl wallpaper.

sleek chic

A homeowner with a can-do attitude combines research and shopping to turn a dated kitchen into a glamorous gathering spot.

before

Beige is like a chef's pure white dish, Des Moines homeowner Karin Edwards says. "Both are the perfect backdrop for whatever you want to show off. And in my kitchen, that's my food and my friends," she says. Karin's sleek beige and white kitchen is indeed a perfect backdrop for good times. It's striking and chic, yet doesn't shout for attention.

Karin's goal when remodeling the room was high style with low fuss—and a modest budget. But high style can come at a cost. Sleek lines meant flush-set appliances, recessed undercabinet lighting, and hidden outlets that aren't typical of an off-the-shelf kitchen. And Karin's budget hovered around $10,000.

Fortunately, the house, a 1950s flat-roof, offered motivation. "It's sited perfectly on a hilltop, with windows on three sides to look out on a sprawling lawn of old oaks," she says. "The views are so stunning, they'd make you take on even the craziest project."

No mistake about it, a true mountain of makeover work was needed to carve this diamond from its rough. The kitchen's layout had not changed since the home was built. A torn linoleum floor, composite cabinets in a faux-oak finish, and cracked laminate countertops remained from a 1970s redo. And to add to the challenge, Karin had left the kitchen for last.

Having renovated every other room with her late husband, a talented do-it-yourselfer, she had to find a low-cost solution to meld with the style of a home with custom walnut built-ins and travertine floors. "The kitchen had to look like the rest of the house and preserve its flow," Karin says. "For two years I kept trying to make revisions to a plan I could no longer afford. In time, I learned that the only way to get the work done was to have some fun with it."

On nights and weekends she loaded up her dachshunds, Mouse and Lefty, for a visit to a home center or to meet contractors. She also brought friends into the act. "Someone has to hold the other end of the tape measure and, for me, that's my friend Sara Risseuw," she says. "The minute I call, she knows I've got another wild idea and need her help to pull it off."

With her friend on board, Karin began simplifying. She chopped the square room into three parts: a tidy galley with only as much prep space as she really needed, a walk-in pantry for extra storage, and a laundry closet for the washer and dryer that used to reside next to the kitchen sink.

"Remember Mrs. C's kitchen on the TV show *Happy Days*?" she says. "I had it. Cabinets on two walls and empty space in the middle. It wasn't a good use of space. A galley is more functional."

The galley was also an economical decision. Karin sliced her cabinetry costs by at least one-third by installing only what she needed—an L shape of two-tone cabinets with upper garage-door-

THIS PHOTO: Homeowner Karin Edwards splurged on a Viking cooktop and oven, but limited costly tilework to behind the cooktop. Stock horizontal cabinets didn't fill the wall space, so Karin left extra space between units and framed them out with beige end panels and mosaic tile, creating a spice cubby. OPPOSITE LEFT: A drop-in sink, laminate countertop, and faucet, all from IKEA, kept the budget down. OPPOSITE RIGHT: Flip-up doors and a glass shelf detail the cabinets.

VIKING
PROFESSIONAL

"Planning a walk-in pantry saved a bunch of money on cabinetry and added a cozy spot for my pup, Mouse."

—HOMEOWNER KARIN EDWARDS

style lift-ups. Anything that doesn't fit can find a home in her walk-in pantry or tall pullout units on the refrigerator wall. "I really like walk-in pantries where you can grab things immediately off the shelves," she says. "There's a ton of storage in very little space. And all it costs is drill-and-hang-yourself wall shelves."

Siting the pantry behind the refrigerator wall also allowed Karin to cheat space from behind to create the luxe look of a flush-set appliance when, in fact, the fridge is much deeper than flanking pullouts. "The cabinet on top of the fridge is even shallower than the pullouts," Karin says. "I had a wood support built behind it. Now all three depths—the fridge and two cabinet types—look equal."

Cabinet doors on the refrigerator wall are glossy white, while the galley's other walls are interspersed white with beige and frosted-glass doors. "One door type seemed boring," Karin says.

She saved money by keeping the plumbing where it had been, running a bit of extra pipe to move the faucet a few inches. That

meant there was no need to break through walls to run pipes or worry about adding insulation.

Still, she needed to cut costs—mostly, to afford her cooking appliances. "Consistency is key in a small space, and I was already using three door types," Karin says. "I couldn't have stainless interrupt their rhythm of beige and white surfaces. I had to have a white cooktop and oven. They had to sit flush and cook as good as they look."

With the cost of appliances, however, it looked like Karin's budget had been blown. "I'd like to think my mom came to the rescue," she says. The daughter of a wallcoverings designer, Karin opted to install a crocodile-texture backsplash made of washable vinyl wallpaper glued to a board and framed with chrome mirror edging. "Sara and I papered the boards together," she says. "It took a half day, no more."

The choice limited costly tile installation to where it was needed—behind the cooktop. Plus the wallpaper's faux-croc texture met Karin's style quotient and synced with the room's silver and gold accents.

"I kept thinking I was doing this for some kind of glamour girl, someone always entertaining," Karin says. In other words, someone just like her.

ABOVE: A small desk provides a spot to plan menus or pay bills. Using a stainless end panel on the adjacent cabinet creates a magnetic surface for hanging notes. ABOVE RIGHT: Pullout pantries mix fixed and movable units that can be accessed from two sides. OPPOSITE: White shelves with stainless-steel frames hang over faux-crocodile wallpaper in the walk-in pantry. Leftover travertine tile from another project clads one wall for extra texture.

details, details

Keeping her eyes on the prize—a pretty kitchen—homeowner Shelley Stewart survives an exhaustive remodeling project. Here's her first-person account.

There's no way I can tell you how many times I went to work thinking I looked OK, only to have someone tell me that I had sawdust on my clothes. Or I would look down to see my new shoes covered with drywall dust. I guess it comes with the territory of being a do-it-yourself-obsessed fanatic.

It all started when I decided to add a combination dining area and TV room to the back of my Des Moines house. I thought, *While I'm doing this, I might as well go on and reconfigure the kitchen.* It seemed so simple, but before it was over I'd learned some tough—and valuable—lessons on remodeling.

RIGHT: When the base cabinet next to the sink didn't provide much countertop space, homeowner Shelley Stewart added open, adjustable shelving to stretch the surface area. Columns and furniturelike feet further the custom look of the kitchen. OPPOSITE: Shelley created an upscale look in her kitchen with creamy white cabinetry that mixes open and closed storage. Special touches include crown molding that blends with the parquet floor.

"Put your money into things that draw attention. Splurge on a stylish faucet or colorful accent tiles."

—HOMEOWNER SHELLEY STEWART

The first contractor was Rick. He arrived with his wife, and somehow their air of respectability convinced me that he was the one to do the job. He left with my down payment of $1,000 and gave me a list of materials to order, promising to return in a few days to start the job. He stressed that he worked fast and would finish by the end of summer, and I believed him.

We agreed that he wouldn't tear out the wall between my kitchen and the addition until the new space was "dried in" (translation: roofed, with exterior walls, windows, and doors in place to keep the weather out) to minimize the mess in the house. Things seemed to go well as he laid out the joists on the foundation. "You want the maximum ceiling height, right?" he asked. We soon realized that the sloped roof I had planned would necessitate relocating the existing upstairs windows. "Oh, no! Construction in the bedrooms, too?" I asked. "Oh, well."

The day he joined the rooflines was a hot one. By late afternoon, when shingles and tar paper had been ripped away, he was exhausted. Heat gave way to rain. By 8 o'clock that night, water was pouring into the house, dripping through the kitchen ceiling onto the countertop, coursing through the living room walls to the basement, where it soaked into books, boxes, and my newly laid laminate "floating floor," which lived up to its name. "Who could have known that we'd have rain?" Rick asked. Anyone who looked at the sky, I thought.

The weather and the house dried out, and the rest of the work went fine—until the day Rick disappeared to start another job. The old exterior wall was still there and my kitchen untouched.

The next contractor, Jack, was recommended by the drywall contractor. He arrived like a leprechaun, almost jumping with excitement at the prospect of tearing out the wall. I watched with amazement as he and his helper took crowbars and hammers to the only barrier left between my kitchen and its new life.

The leprechaun wasted no time ripping out old fixtures, appliances, and cabinets, too. I wasn't ready to lose my sink yet. "Look," he barked, "do you want us to do the job or not?" "Well, yes," I said. "I'll just cook in the microwave and wash dishes in the upstairs bathroom."

Within two days, I had strong suspicions that there was more to Jack's hyperactivity than excitement over my kitchen. When he started showing up late and couldn't remember conversations we had just the day before, I told him to leave. The home improvement store had already delivered the drywall and other items Jack had ordered, so there I was—$2,000 worth of material in my driveway, rain forecast in two days, and no contractor.

A friend of a friend knew someone who was supposed to be really, really good at remodeling. This time, it was true! Rod came in when I didn't know which way to turn. He owns a contracting company, his employees (Rich and Kenny) were pros, and his subcontractors were the best.

Rod's crew shifted the wall between the kitchen and the living room, closing a door in the process. A plumber installed the new gas line for the cooktop and water pipes for a second sink. An electrician came by to do the wiring, adding downlights.

Finally, I was ready to starting putting my kitchen back together. Explaining that my hodgepodge of cabinets, including some from garage sales, would create an elegant "unfitted look" at a fraction of the cost for all-new ones, I convinced Rod that they would fit the space (and crossed my fingers that they would). One secondhand cabinet, capped with the shop-class workbench top I

Custom-Look Cabinets

Homeowner Shelley Stewart originally had a quote for cabinets from a home center for $15,000. She was able to spend less than $3,500 by doing some smart shopping and adding details.

MIX MASTERED Shelley used some cabinets from the original kitchen, but she also found cabinets at a local Habitat for Humanity ReStore, in a classified ad, and at a garage sale. With a rough layout in mind, she bought the used cabinets and hoped for the best. She hired carpenters to install them, and she painted them to unify the look.

PERSONALLY TAILORED Shelley didn't settle for the status quo with her cabinets. To add interest to the range area, she added a half-column, *below left*. Slide-out shelves, *below right*, increase storage capacity in cabinets in the peninsula.

OPPOSITE: Teal-green tile on the countertops provides an unexpected splash of color. For continuity, the tile repeats on the backsplash and the focal-point mosaic behind the cooktop. Antiqued-copper knobs on the cabinets add a flourish.

before

found at an online auction site, became a peninsula; two barstools added seating for a casual dining spot.

I bought my appliances and sink locally after online research, saving money on discontinued models. I saved by ordering the faucet for the double-bowl sink online, and used the old one for the smaller sink.

Stacking everything in the living room until we were ready for it became an issue. For months the only place I could sit, even for meals, was either at my desk chair or on my bed. By now, it was the middle of winter, which meant freezing cold and snow. All sawing for both the kitchen and the addition had to be done inside. One word suffices: dust.

And so it went. It seemed as if every time I earned a nickel, I spent 6 cents on supplies. The construction crew left, and I was alone in the unfinished kitchen.

I proceeded to prime, sand, paint, sand, paint again, sand again, and paint again until the cabinets, which came from five different sources, looked as if they were meant to go together.

By buying my oak parquet flooring a few packs at a time, I softened the financial impact. When finally installing it in the kitchen and adjoining family room, I found that I needed more, and discovered to my horror that it had been discontinued. I drove

ABOVE LEFT: **The microwave is at eye level so it's easy to access.** ABOVE: **Open shelves display collectibles and everyday dishes.** OPPOSITE: **Closing a doorway created room for a new cooktop and mosaic backsplash. The cabinets are a budget-smart mix of old and new. The peninsula top was salvaged from a workbench.**

like a maniac to home improvement stores in Kansas City and Omaha and bought all they had, ending up with a little more than I needed, but who cared? I had finished the floor. It wasn't all that hard, but the gunky brown adhesive does stick—to everything.

To inject some color, I decided to use 18-inch squares of teal-green tile with inserts of green tumbled marble on the countertops. Creating the design as I went was half the fun, and a good wet-saw made short work of cutting all those little pieces.

As soon as the countertops were in place, Rod's crew returned to install the appliances and connect the sink. Soon after, I was arranging drawers, putting things on shelves, and (hurray, hurray!) properly cooking and washing dishes once again. I survived, and I have a beautiful kitchen to show for it!

THIS PHOTO: **Cherry cabinetry enriches the look of this kitchen. Glass upper cabinets echo the detailing on the windows.** OPPOSITE: **Stainless-steel appliances brighten the cooking area.**

warm embrace

With an abundance of rich wood, this kitchen has stay-awhile appeal.

Small touches make a big difference. The homeowners of this Chicago-area bungalow realized that a few months after their kitchen renovation was complete—or they thought it was complete. After their daughter spilled grape juice on the base of the breakfast bar, leaving a purple stain on the drywall, they called kitchen designer Catherine Heir back to assess the damage. Call it a happy accident. Heir paneled the base so it would be easier to wipe down and also blend with the room's cherry cabinetry. "That small touch really completed the kitchen," Heir says.

Now, the finished-off kitchen has it all—traditional richness that complements the character of the home and everyday ease that suits a family of four. "You have to be able to meld function with the pretty," Heir says. "This is a family kitchen, not a showpiece kitchen. Even though it looks nice, it needs to function really well."

ABOVE RIGHT: **Clay pots are an earthy complement to the tumbled marble backsplash. "We wanted something on that wall that was modern yet understated," kitchen designer Catherine Heir says. "The brick fits the style of the house."** RIGHT: **The faucet and soap dispenser suit the room's traditional look.** OPPOSITE: **A wall of cabinetry incorporates a message center, the microwave oven (with an appliance garage under it), and the refrigerator.**

A mix of different-size drawers provides keep-it-organized storage for small and large items.

It took a few design tricks to make that functionality a reality. A big challenge was the layout. The family had been making do with a traffic-blocking table in the center of the room, and they were hoping an island with stools could be worked in instead. "I tried, but it just proved impossible to fit a practical island with seating into this kitchen," Heir says. Instead, she added a small island, then removed the wall to the dining room to allow space for a breakfast bar. "This gave them a place to sit—plus it visually enlarged both rooms and brought natural light into the kitchen," she says.

The island, used as a baking station, mixes open and closed storage. Pots, pans, and spices are housed on the side facing the range; cookbooks and collectibles have a home on open shelves visible upon entering the room.

The play between pretty and practical shows in other areas too. The raised breakfast bar, with quartz-surfacing, hides the work area, including the sink. The sink itself is a deep one-bowl model, chosen to help hide dirty dishes when the homeowner, an avid cook, doesn't have time to tend to them immediately.

The tumbled marble backsplash that the homeowners loved but didn't think would be functional was sealed and enhanced so it holds its own against spills and stains. "It helps protect it from flying spaghetti sauce," Heir says.

The homeowners' flexibility was another key to Heir being able to work in everything they wanted. An area originally planned for a desk morphed into a storage-packed message center with drawers assigned to each family member. "As the kitchen progressed and we decided to take out the wall, the homeowner decided she'd sit at the breakfast bar instead of a desk," Heir says. In another shift, a short walkway to a porch that was demolished became a walk-in pantry.

"It was hugely important to maximize every nook and cranny," Heir says. "This kitchen is a nice blend of function and style. It's the heart of the home."

RIGHT: **Space-saving double pocket doors close off the pantry, which formerly was a walkway to an unusable porch.** BELOW: **Draperies on the new French doors dress up the dining room. The chandelier is from the same collection as the kitchen fixtures—an easy way to give the two spaces design continuity.** OPPOSITE: **The raised breakfast bar, detailed with curved brackets, hides kitchen messes.**

THIS PHOTO: **Classic columns detail the breakfast bar, an extension of the sink countertop.**

OPPOSITE: **Decorative brackets give the illusion of supporting upper cabinets.**

glass act

Never mind the daily chores. This kitchen's lightness lets calm prevail, even when the dishes (or laundry) call.

Architects Stuart Cohen and Julie Hacker learned what it's like to be clients when they updated the kitchen of their Chicago-area home. As they made design decisions, they found themselves borrowing their favorite features from clients' homes. "Many architects build as a way for them to experiment and show clients what they can do," Stuart says. "This kitchen is the opposite. It has things in it we liked that we've done for other people."

The idea of adding a storage closet to the modest-size kitchen, part of a condominium in a 100-year-old building, led to a full-fledged redo. The couple kept the U-shape layout but changed the positions of fixtures and appliances to improve views and function. "By moving things around, we allotted ourselves a lot more counter space," Julie says.

Wood cabinetry, painted a warm white, sets a classic tone for the kitchen, replacing cheap laminate cabinets Stuart had installed in the late 1970s, before marrying Julie. "He was a single parent with no money," Julie explains. A bank of glass-front upper units is the room's distinguishing feature. "When you walk in from the dining room, you see an entire wall of glass-front cabinetry," Julie says. "I think it's very dramatic. And of course glass cabinets always make a room feel a bit larger." Stuart adds, "We also wanted the reflectivity of the glass."

New sills and brackets beneath the upper cabinets provide the architectural detailing common to homes of the era. "Brackets are kind of a signature piece for us," Stuart says. "We have an architect's fetish, a pet peeve about things that look like they're not held up by anything."

ABOVE: **A stacked washer/dryer combo hides behind tall cabinet doors at the left end of the range wall.** OPPOSITE: **A six-burner range with matching hood complements the proportions of the high-ceilinged room. "The four-burner range looked silly, like a child's toy—visually too small for the space," homeowner Stuart Cohen says.**

White subway tile on backsplashes imparts vintage style amid modern ease. "When you go into really old houses, every surface in the kitchen is tile," Stuart says. "I think it had to do with being able to scrub it all down. It's easy to keep clean."

But there's nothing old-school about the room's sleek appliances. A professional-grade range with matching hood replaced a peninsula-mounted cooktop and broken double oven. Julie, a triathlete, had found a practical use for the dormant oven. "I would hang bathing suits on it," she says. The sink is a deep pro-style model. "You can put your dishes in there and you can't even see them," Julie says. The refrigerator and microwave oven also have an out-of-the-way home—in a retrofitted hallway that leads to the dining room.

Julie's favorite utilitarian feature, though, is the stacked washer/dryer combo incorporated into the cabinetry near the range. Now, Julie can do laundry and kitchen chores at the same time. "Having the washer/dryer in the kitchen makes life easier for me," she says. And having such a well-appointed space in which to do laundry—or any chore—also makes life more enjoyable.

ABOVE LEFT: **A shapely bridge faucet teams with a dispenser for instant hot water and filtered cold water.** ABOVE: **Moving small appliances and the refrigerator to a walk-through annex to the dining room freed up space in the kitchen. "It works for our lifestyle,"** Stuart says. OPPOSITE: **The doorway frames an impressive view of glass-front cabinetry and cashmere white granite countertops. A botanical-pattern wallpaper on the wall near the sink complements the natural colors in the countertops.**

open
horizons

3

The walls are coming down in today's kitchens. The open plan concept, where the kitchen flows into a dining room or family room, is a big boon to a small space. Suddenly, a tight-fit kitchen seems bigger and more livable. But it's not just about gaining square footage— real or perceived. Connectivity is driving the trend toward openness. As the homeowners of these featured kitchens discovered, a wide-open room encourages mingling with family members and makes it easier to accommodate guests who inevitably end up in the kitchen.

How far you want to take it is up to you. Simply removing a bank of upper cabinets that blocks the view into a dining area can make your kitchen more welcoming. Widening a narrow doorway has a similar effect, allowing cooks to savor some semi-privacy. The main thing is to open yourself up to the possibilities so you can make an informed decision about what works best for your home and your lifestyle.

Cabinets detailed with crown molding and glass doors make for a pretty view when people sit at the peninsula or are in the adjoining dining room.

tailored for today

An era-sensitive addition brings a family of four together in their kitchen.

It's amazing what the right kitchen can do for a home—and a family. Sherri Teague discovered that when she and her husband, Richard, added on to their San Diego home to gain a better-functioning kitchen and a bit more living space. After making do with a cramped one-cook kitchen in their 1920s Tudor-style home, the couple and their two children finally had a welcoming gathering hub. "Our new kitchen has a come-and-hang-out feel," Sherri says. "My husband can be cooking dinner, our twins can be doing homework or art projects at the peninsula, and I can be making cupcakes for a school fund-raiser—all at the same time."

The Teagues' newfound quality time didn't require a lot of quantity. By today's standards, the kitchen is still modestly sized. The room's long, narrow shape is reminiscent of the home's original galley-style kitchen, but the two spaces couldn't be more different. The old kitchen was an introvert that kept the cook isolated. The new kitchen is an extrovert; it's all about openness and mingling. Instead of an interior wall, a peninsula is the only separation between the kitchen and adjoining dining room that flows into a family room.

While the open plan makes the kitchen seem larger, windows that let in abundant natural light play a space-enhancing role too. "We wanted great light and windows on both sides of the room to look out over the gardens," Sherri says. French doors and transom

windows in the adjoining dining room draw in even more light and also allow a wide view to the backyard.

For the Teagues, a modern kitchen didn't mean sacrificing character. "We absolutely love the details of older homes," Sherri says. Architects Ione Stiegler and Joseph Reid, both experienced in historic preservation, took care to blend the addition with the original part of the home. Arches—seen in a niche above the range and dining room doorway—play off the shape of the home's windows. The kitchen's tray ceiling replicates the ceiling that was in the original dining room. Schoolhouse pendants and a farmhouse sink lend vintage charm. "Our greatest challenge was finding the right materials that fit the couple's needs and the style of the home," Reid says.

ABOVE LEFT: **With feet detailing it, the sink cabinet resembles a piece of furniture.** ABOVE: **Durable soapstone countertops are part of the kitchen's timeless black-and-white scheme.** OPPOSITE TOP, LEFT: **Glass knobs and subway tile add vintage flair.** OPPOSITE BOTTOM, LEFT: **The tiled niche complements the facade of the living room fireplace.** OPPOSITE RIGHT: **The reproduction Heartland Legend range that is the centerpiece of the kitchen has modern bells and whistles.**

The soapstone countertops that are one of Sherri's favorite features fill the bill. They're durable, low maintenance, and period appropriate. "Soapstone was used quite frequently in homes built around the same time as this house, and it works perfectly with the white subway tile backsplash," Reid says. "The soapstone is one of the room's most stunning features." Equally eye-catching is the reproduction range Sherri found by searching the Internet. "I wanted something that looked old but functioned perfectly," she says.

These days, Sherri says pretty much everything in her kitchen is working perfectly—and looking better than she imagined it could. The space is so inviting that the family no longer makes a beeline out of it as soon as the dishes are done. "Our kitchen is definitely like a second family room," Sherri says.

Room for Improvement

Whether you're adding on to your home or gutting an existing kitchen, consider these tips before you launch your project.

DON'T OVERDO Spending no more than 15 percent of your home's value is a good guideline for kitchen remodeling. Spend more than that, and you risk losing money when you sell.

PLAN FOR EXCESS The unexpected is bound to happen with any home improvement project. Make sure your budget has wiggle room. Allot extra when ordering materials, too. One builder suggests ordering 5 to 10 percent more flooring than you think you need. And hold on to scraps; you never know when you'll need another little piece.

DO IT IN STAGES If you can't afford your entire dream kitchen up front, target the more permanent elements first. This includes structural changes, flooring, and cabinetry. Choose affordable temporary solutions for appliances, faucets, and sinks—or use what you have. You can swap those out later without disrupting the entire room.

Light fixtures are a simple way to add interest. In an open room, mix styles to define spaces and set a mood.

RIGHT: The new kitchen flows into a spacious dining room. The arched doorway echoes the details in the old part of the home. BELOW: Chandeliers and ceiling beams bring interest overhead. OPPOSITE LEFT: The kitchen draws natural light from the dining room's windows and French doors. Abundant glass also makes it easy to keep tabs on kids playing in the backyard. OPPOSITE RIGHT: Gridded glass-front cabinet doors play off the window panes.

A two-level peninsula that replaced a wall made this kitchen seem larger. At the opposite end of the room, a shallow countertop provides an extra work space.

perfect harmony

Removing a wall and playing up a fresh mix of modern
and old-fashioned looks update a bungalow's hub.

Design inspiration sometimes comes from unlikely sources—such as a few small bowls. The bowls, which a Toronto couple found in a home accessories store (and still use), cued the fresh cream-and-green palette of their remodeled kitchen. "We always tell clients to find something they love and build off it," says designer Sarah Richardson, who worked on the 1920s bungalow space with associate designer Kate Stuart.

The striped bowls had a clean-lined, modern sensibility that the couple loved—and found lacking in their existing kitchen. The room had a mishmash of original cabinets and 1960s add-ons, as well as scant counter space, awkwardly placed appliances, and bad lighting. "It was your typical time-warp vintage kitchen," Richardson says. "It felt cramped and cut off from the living and dining rooms. The only good thing was that it was so bad that there was no need to try and salvage a single thing."

Richardson's first recommendation was dramatic—and, for the couple, a little scary. She suggested they take down the wall between the small kitchen and the adjacent dining room and replace it with a multipurpose peninsula. At first, the homeowners were reluctant to lose formal dining space, but eliminating the wall turned out to be one of their best decisions. "The house gets great western light, but none of it could filter through to brighten the kitchen before," Richardson says. "Removing the wall really changed the whole feel of the house."

ABOVE LEFT: Placing the stainless-steel refrigerator, matching double oven, and hardworking pantry cabinetry on the same interior wall frees exterior walls for windows and long sections of counter space. LEFT: A tall stack of open shelves next to the refrigerator breaks up the expanse of cabinetry and shows off a collection of 1960s dishware. OPPOSITE: Old-fashioned marble countertops and crystal knobs work well with a modern glass-tile backsplash. The striped bowls stacked on the countertop to the left of the sink inspired the kitchen's cream-and-green color palette. The peninsula's upper level is an eating bar.

In another bold move, Richardson combined a small pantry with closet space from an adjacent bedroom to create a long wall for the refrigerator, double oven, and pantry. "I'm a big fan of entire walls being dedicated to a combination of full-height pantries, appliances, and open display," Richardson says. She also opened a back staircase near the kitchen to allow better access to all the storage.

With the space issues solved, Richardson worked her magic with surfaces and materials. Stained wood cabinets had the potential to close the kitchen back in, so she opted for soft green cabinetry that keeps things light and airy. Marble countertops and stainless-steel appliances are complemented by a backsplash of shimmering glass tile. The tile is a modern touch that now ranks as one of the couple's favorite features.

Richardson says adding modern materials in modest doses helped blur the lines between vintage and contemporary in the bungalow kitchen. "We wanted the kitchen's architecture to be right for the period of the home, but we wanted colors, accents, and accessories to be more modern," she says. "Our goal was a contemporary and updated kitchen that complemented the cottagey 1920s home and reflected the homeowners' casual lifestyle."

UNITED STATE
Removing a wall between the kitchen and dining room allows two modest-size spaces to function as one large gathering place.

TOP LEFT: Like the sleek hood above it, the countertop in the cooking area is stainless steel. Keeping the cooktop separate from the ovens helps multiple cooks work in a small space. MIDDLE LEFT: The creamy cabinets feature recessed panels with beaded edges, a classic look that reflects the home's 1920s roots. LEFT: The fresh color scheme would be the apple of anyone's eye. OPPOSITE: The dining room, once isolated from the kitchen, now shares its natural light and soft colors.

An open layout gives this rich-looking kitchen a more contemporary look. The compact island works well in the two-person kitchen.

nested
interest

A couple starting a new
chapter in life embrace
uptown style and ease.

Nearing retirement age, with their
children grown and out of the house, Debbie and
Ken Porter traded their reproduction Early American
saltbox on 5 acres in rural Maine for low-maintenance
townhome living closer to the nearby city of Portland.
"We wanted something new," Debbie says. "With the
kids gone, we were ready for a change."

In changing addresses, the couple also changed
kitchen styles. Since they were starting a new chapter
in their lives, they decided it was the ideal time to
adopt a contemporary look that was new to them.
Designer Chris Coyle satisfied Debbie and Ken's
desire for an open layout that would be efficient for
two people yet offer potential for entertaining. At the
same time, he melded some urban edginess into the
couple's more traditional design tastes.

The loft-style floor plan leaves the kitchen open
to the main living areas, including an adjacent dining
room, where tall bay windows supply a wealth of
natural light. A two-level peninsula straddles the
kitchen and dining room, providing a spot for casual
meals or bar service. Although the kitchen was too
narrow for a full island, a small, movable table adds an
extra bit of work space and also serves as a buffet.

Although contemporary style and lofts
themselves can sometimes look cold, Coyle made sure
this kitchen was warm and inviting. The space is a sea

of rich wood, which reflects the couple's traditional tastes. Clean-lined, black-glazed cherry cabinetry sets an uptown tone. "We wanted the cabinetry to be really different," Ken says. The cabinets are paired with countertops of Venetian Gold granite, a striking stone with purple and olive flecks.

Those colors repeat in the glass-mosaic-tile backsplash, along with metallic hues that match the sheen of stainless-steel appliances and cabinetry pulls. Red birch flooring grounds the entire scheme in traditional warmth.

Although Debbie and Ken no longer have children at home, their new nest is far from empty—the kitchen is full of interest and inspiration for all.

ABOVE LEFT: Venetian Gold granite counters provide contemporary color and pattern in a traditional surface. The edge treatment smoothly marks a change in countertop depth at the cooktop. ABOVE: A high-style hood calls attention to the low-profile cooktop, as does a glass-mosaic-tile backsplash. LEFT: A double oven and microwave complete the cooking zone. Stainless-steel fronts stand out against black-glazed cherry cabinets, while cabinet pulls mimic the oven-door handles. OPPOSITE: Designer Chris Coyle varied cabinet heights and depths throughout the kitchen, creating contemporary-style motion and perspective.

Clean lines, fresh colors, and cottage charm bring an East Coast feeling to this Minneapolis kitchen. The kitchen flows into a sitting area that opens to a small deck with a commanding view.

city cottage

The spirit of an old Nantucket beach house pervades the kitchen of a new metropolitan home in the Midwest.

Shelves stretch across windows, providing display space without blocking sight lines.

Serendipity smiled on a couple when they spotted an empty lot for sale near their home. After renovating two previous homes in their Minneapolis neighborhood, Jeff Junkins and Mike Dillon were ready to take on new construction. Jeff, a designer, knew he wanted to incorporate elements found in coastal cottages and farmhouses.

"We wanted to bring in that East Coast feeling," Jeff says. "The house is on a steep hill, so we designed the home so you enter the first floor below the main living space to avoid climbing so many stairs." Architect Ron Brenner and builders from Cottagewood Partners helped Jeff and Mike execute their ideas beautifully. "It's a very cottagey kind of home with a clean and simple design," Brenner says.

The upper-level kitchen, which incorporates a sitting area, is the heart of the home. The open, airy space is perfect for relaxing after a long day at work. It also satisfies the couple's yen for small-group entertaining. Guests can hang out around the island, which features a built-in wine rack, or sit in the comfortable chairs in the sitting area and still chat with the cook. A wall-mount TV is visible from both spots.

LEFT: The homeowners squeezed two little luxuries into their kitchen: a second sink that can be used for prepping foods or as a bar area and a wall-mount TV. OPPOSITE: Simple recessed-panel cabinetry and easy-to-maintain flagstone flooring keep the kitchen casual.

Thoughtful details—some decorative, others functional—bring a small kitchen to life.

A 10-foot-wide doorway allows an easy flow into the adjoining living room, contributing to the kitchen's sense of spaciousness. A charming deck accessible from the kitchen stretches square footage to the outdoors. In warm weather, Jeff and Mike enjoy morning coffee on the deck or a glass of wine there at sunset. "It's ideal for watching the weather roll in because of the extended view," Jeff says. The couple also greet visitors from the deck, which overlooks the front of the home.

The west-facing deck pours light into the kitchen, as do windows on the south-facing appliance wall, warming the Chilton flagstone floor. "The floor is easy to maintain and clean," Jeff says.

He notes how the blue in the rustic stone complements the painted walls. And the sea-inspired tones blend with the soft green of the island. Mike, who likes modern touches, especially appreciates the stainless-steel appliances and matching subway tile backsplash. "What we like about the kitchen is what we like about the whole house: It's a nice blend of our styles," Jeff says.

ABOVE: The sitting area, with two chairs facing the kitchen, recalls an old-style keeping room. OPPOSITE TOP, LEFT: Gracefully curved brackets detail the cabinets. OPPOSITE TOP, RIGHT: A removable shelf below the built-in microwave doubles as a cutting board. OPPOSITE BOTTOM, LEFT: A window shelf provides clever display space. OPPOSITE BOTTOM, RIGHT: Granite countertops have a marblelike appearance. Because the kitchen had only one usable wall, the island needed to be a workhorse. It houses the main sink, the dishwasher, and a wine rack.

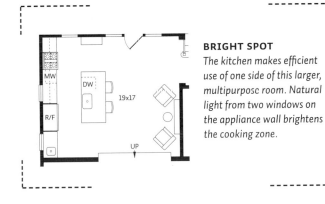

BRIGHT SPOT
The kitchen makes efficient use of one side of this larger, multipurpose room. Natural light from two windows on the appliance wall brightens the cooking zone.

Interior designer Carla Kantola indulged her taste for modern kitchen style without souring the charm of her 1930s home in Dallas.

passing through

This kitchen is a center of attention. One end flows into the dining area and the other opens to the family room.

Although she's a modernist at heart, interior designer Carla Kantola knew anything too sleek would look out of place in her 1936 cottage-style home in Dallas. So when Carla and her husband, Bill, updated the kitchen, she chose its contemporary elements with care. "I wanted it as modern as possible without looking severe," she says.

With help from designer Brooke Bodenheimer, a member of the National Kitchen & Bath Association (NKBA), Carla changed the look and layout. See-through upper cabinets on one wall are a creative way to boost storage without blocking off the adjacent family room. "I love that the kitchen is very open to the family room," Carla says. "When we entertain, we don't feel closed-off in the kitchen."

On the opposite side of the room, the kitchen dissolves into the dining area. There, a round table placed near a cushioned window seat is a contemporary spin on a traditional banquette.

In the heart of the kitchen, the cooking core also required some shifts, starting with the refrigerator. "The door barely opened without hitting the island," Carla says. "So we relocated it to a more open space."

The cooktop shifted from the island to the along the room's perimeter. "There wasn't a lot of space to place pots or bowls around the cooktop, so we decided to make the island more of a work surface," Carla says.

> **"I love that the kitchen is very open to the family room.
> When we entertain, we don't feel closed off in the kitchen."**
> —HOMEOWNER CARLA KANTOLA

Both Carla and Bill cook, so they added a sink to the island. "With two sinks, we can work without getting in each other's way," Carla says. The sinks feature square basins and clean-lined faucets. Equally sleek are the pro-grade stainless-steel appliances. "Appliances aren't just for looks in our kitchen," Carla says. "We really use them."

Granite counters are a classic choice, but their thick edges are modern. "I fell in love with this granite," Carla says. "The minute it caught my eye, I knew it was the one I wanted. I like the lightness of its color."

Maple cabinets toe the line between traditional and contemporary. Because the room has only one window, Carla chose a light color. "I didn't want the room to feel like a cave," she says. "We used a darker wood finish on the island for an added accent and more of a furniture feel." The cabinets contain lots of pullouts, fold-outs, and deep shelves. "Since the kitchen is fairly small, storage was critical," Carla says.

All the updates—from the openness to the efficient layout—have made the kitchen a much more inspired, and inspiring, space. "It's now a pleasant place to spend time," Carla says.

Take-Home Tip
Edge treatments can make standard-thickness granite slabs look beefier, which gives the classic stone a contemporary look.

ABOVE: On the wall adjoining the family room, see-through upper cabinets provide glassware storage without blocking light. Near the island, wall ovens are surrounded by pantry cabinets.
OPPOSITE: Both the professional-grade cooktop and the clean-lined cabinetry provide the modern look Carla wanted for her remodeled kitchen without disowning the home's cottage roots.

TOP LEFT: The sink window reflects 1930s architecture, but it's framed by contemporary glass mosaic tile. TOP RIGHT: A built-in coffeemaker is mounted conveniently above the microwave. "It's like having your own Starbucks," Carla says. ABOVE LEFT: Bianco Murano granite countertops bring out the kitchen's softer, vintage-look side. ABOVE: The two-way upper cabinets between the kitchen and family room feature ribbed glass. OPPOSITE: A fresh palette and sleek furniture update the dining area. The hardwood floor is rich with tradition yet looks contemporary.

age appropriate

In this vintage seaside retreat, opening up comes by simply lifting original porch shutters.

It only seems natural that this Bell Island home located along the cool waters of Long Island Sound on the Connecticut coast would reflect its seaside surroundings. Previous remodels stripped some original charm from the 1928 home, but the most recent renovation restored its cozy coastal character and also opened rooms to sunshine and striking views of the water.

Although openness was one of the goals, the homeowners knew when to say when. A modern layout, where the kitchen, living room, and dining room are one space, just wouldn't have felt right for the old home. On the flip side, a kitchen that was cut off from the action—and those water views—seemed an injustice. The best-of-both-worlds solution came not by knocking down a wall but by flipping up a shutter. A wide shutter on an interior wall was pulled up and mounted to the ceiling, providing a large cutout that opens the kitchen to the living room and the views beyond. The shutter recalls the days when the living room was a porch and gives the renovated home a connection to its past.

Attaching the shutter to the ceiling opens this coastal kitchen to the living room, which was originally a porch. Mirror-backed shelves line the walls, bouncing light around.

Beaded-board backsplashes play up the nautical theme that runs throughout the home. For design continuity and to keep things casual, beaded-board wainscoting details the living room. Built-in shelves in the living room display porcelain and ironstone collections. In the kitchen, a collection of porcelain plates garners attention.

The homeowners found that borrowing space from unused rooms and adding storage improved the home's layout without altering its footprint. New painted Shaker-style cabinets provide storage space in the kitchen. A renovated utility room a few steps up from the kitchen now functions as a well-appointed butler's pantry. Beefed-up baseboards, crown moldings, and trim add strong architectural interest. The most interesting feature, though, is the shutter between the kitchen and living room, and also one on a built-in bar. They're reminders that this is, and always will be, an old summer house where life is meant to be casual and carefree.

ABOVE LEFT: **Inspired by boat interiors, a bar near the living room boasts a cherry wood counter with a marine finish. Beaded-board wainscoting, a repeated element throughout the house, wraps around the bar.** ABOVE: **Ceiling beams draw the eye out of the kitchen and into the living room—a design sleight of hand that seems to stretch both rooms.** OPPOSITE: **Set against a backdrop of creamy white cabinets and a beaded-board backsplash, the white-and-blue porcelain in the kitchen takes center stage. Ribbed glass in the cabinet doors has a wavy look that's a subtle play on the home's coastal location. It's also a period-appropriate touch.**

dream rooms, real budgets

4

Beautiful kitchens are easy to come by these days. Flip through a magazine or cable channels, and there they are—yours for the dreaming. Well, how about making those dreams a reality? The homeowners featured on the following pages did just that. Whereas they once had kitchens they simply tolerated, they now have ones they thoroughly enjoy—and they did it without endless budgets.

If you need justification beyond pure pleasure to commit to a makeover, consider this: A remodeled kitchen increases the value of your entire home. Even if you plan to do some of the work yourself, tapping a kitchen design professional before you jump in tends to be a good investment. A pro can help you make sense of an inefficient layout or guide you to surfaces that have lasting appeal. The ultimate goal is simple: You and your kitchen should be a perfect fit.

A rearranged floor plan that includes a peninsula and a new, bigger window makes this kitchen seem larger even though the footprint remained the same.

overdue update

Should they stay or should they go? After debating that question, these homeowners stayed put and remodeled their outmoded kitchen. Now that their home has an inviting new hub, any lingering thoughts about moving have disappeared.

Fed up with the dated kitchen they had lived with for more than 30 years, Penny and Jim Dennison were ready to move. But when they realized how much they loved their neighborhood in Yarmouth, Maine, and their 1970s ranch-style home where they raised two kids, they decided the dated kitchen had to go, not them. On a friend's recommendation, the couple turned to kitchen designer Sarah Steinberg for help with the budget-conscious redesign.

Besides inefficient cabinets, worn counters, and a chipped white tile floor that showed off dirt, Penny and Jim felt hemmed in by the 120-square-foot layout. To make the kitchen seem bigger and more connected to the living room and entry, Steinberg replaced a doorway with an oversize opening. Keeping a few feet

before

Take-Home Tip
To save on labor, keep plumbing fixtures in the same spot when rearranging your kitchen's layout.

> ## "When I walk in every morning I think, *I love this kitchen*. It made us want to stay."
> —HOMEOWNER PENNY DENNISON

of the wall resulted in big savings on the remodel. Stools fit comfortably around a new dining peninsula, a wish-list item after living for years with just a small counter. "I told Jim I had the perfect seat for him," Steinberg says. "Now he can open the refrigerator and watch TV in the living room at the same time."

A vaulted ceiling adds volume and allows for taller wall cabinets, increasing storage and display options. To create a brighter space, Steinberg more than doubled the size of the window above the sink. Stretching the window closer to the counter adds to the spacious look. "Everything we did was to give the illusion of space," Steinberg says.

Next Steinberg fine-tuned the kitchen's L-shape configuration. To save on plumbing costs, she left the sink where it was but replaced it with an undermount stainless-steel model. The range moved to an outside wall, satisfying Penny's request for exterior ventilation. The refrigerator shifted right, making room for a larger model and a pantry cabinet. "Now I can stand in my kitchen and do all my cooking and hardly move," Penny says.

With the kitchen now on display, the old painted cabinets had to go. White birch was a green choice because it's both sustainably harvested and formaldehyde-free.

ABOVE RIGHT: **The range was moved to an exterior wall so it could be vented easily.** OPPOSITE: **Flat, recessed door panels on the cabinets, hammered hardware, and iron trim on the pendants create a transitional look in the kitchen.**

Live Large
Kitchen designer Sarah Steinberg offers the following tips for making the most of a small kitchen.

- Widen door openings to make a room feel more spacious without the expense of removing a wall.

- Enlarge windows. Natural light and views give a room the illusion of more space.

- Stretch cabinetry to the ceiling. Besides making a ceiling feel higher, you gain storage space.

- Choose a light, warm color palette.

- Focus on a few unique decorative elements. "Too many accents and accessories make a room feel cluttered and closed in," Steinberg says.

- Design efficient storage to maximize counter space and create a clutter-free look.

LEFT: A section of 24-inch-deep cabinets surround the refrigerator, creating the look of a built-in unit. BELOW: Keeping the sink in its original location ensures a backyard view. BOTTOM: The new peninsula provides extra storage and serves as a casual eating area.

The peninsula packs in valuable storage and provides a large work counter. "You always need one big area where you can really spread out," Steinberg says. Pewter-finish hardware gives the cabinetry a distinctive look at minimal expense.

Penny's favorite piece of furniture, a red Chinese secretary in the adjacent dining room, inspired accents of red in the kitchen. Steinberg found a one-of-a-kind glass tile with the perfect hint of red for the backsplash. "I always like to find something special," Steinberg says.

While the couple briefly considered concrete counters, they chose granite. They shopped around to find a color they liked at a reasonable price. "Flexibility is key if you want to save money," Steinberg says.

Before the remodel, a change of address seemed imminent. Now, with a spacious-feeling kitchen as efficient as it is beautiful, the couple are happy they stayed put. "When I walk in every morning I think, *I love this kitchen,*" Penny says. "It made us want to stay."

1. THE PERFECT VIEW
A 75×40-inch window replaced a 43×33-inch window to maximize natural light in the kitchen and open up the room.

2. SHIFTED APPLIANCES
The range was relocated to an exterior wall for better ventilation. The refrigerator moved to make room for a pantry cabinet. The sink location stayed the same to save on plumbing.

3. EXTRA EFFICIENCY
A peninsula adds storage and work space. With stools pulled up, it provides in-kitchen seating.

4. ENLARGED WALKWAYS
The doorway to the family room more than tripled in size. The new cased opening gives the kitchen a more spacious feel without adding square footage.

$ budget breakdown

APPLIANCES	
Dishwasher	598
Range	1,169
Refrigerator	1,198
Vent hood	899
CABINETRY	
Cabinetry	10,937
Hardware	300
PLUMBING	
Faucet	282
Instant hot water	305
Sink	636
Sink plug	129
SURFACES	
Backsplash tile	1,504
Countertop	4,180
MISCELLANEOUS	
Lighting	1,957
Miscellaneous	1,000
TOTAL	**$25,094**

ABOVE LEFT: The focal tile, between the range and vent hood, is surrounded by less-expensive slate field tile.

ABOVE RIGHT: The couple trimmed costs by limiting the kitchen to three pendants. For additional lighting, they installed less-expensive undercabinet strips.

White cabinets, frosted-glass door panels, neutral-hue countertops, and stainless-steel appliances all contribute to the light, bright look in this kitchen.

kitchen by the sea

Location, location, location. Heeding those real-estate words of wisdom, a couple buys a lackluster house near the ocean. With an eye for design, the homeowners give the kitchen a one-of-a-kind coastal-inspired makeover that includes real shells embedded in the backsplash.

A home by the sea was always the goal for Jolee and Larry Pink. When they cast their net in the San Diego area and snagged a 1980s house in nearby Encinitas, it seemed their ship had come in.

The 1,800-square-foot house offered a great view and was near the beach. It had a garage large enough to convert into a ceramic studio, where Jolee, owner of an eco-friendly design firm, could fashion tile that would mimic the nearby ocean scene. Alas, paradise was not perfect; the Pinks' new abode was a conventional cookie-cutter home. Recognizing that this was the trade-off required to make seaside living a reality, the couple moved in—with a plan.

Because both Jolee and Larry are handy and skilled at home improvement, they were confident

before

Take-Home Tip
To get a good deal on appliances, look for discontinued models or ones that have minor imperfections, or shop a closing sale.

> **"The new kitchen has changed our lifestyle. And Larry was so inspired that he signed up for cooking school!"**
>
> —HOMEOWNER JOLEE PINK

they could transform the 115-square-foot kitchen into something more than a ho-hum boxy space—and stick to a tight budget. "My first impression was that this is a pretty good, basic kitchen," Jolee says. "The kitchen triangle worked well. There was a large, though unattractive, window with a view of the garden. And although the appliances were outdated and the cabinetry was standard, plain-Jane white, it was a functional space."

Jolee quickly zeroed in on her biggest challenge—transforming what felt like a closed-in kitchen into an open, inviting space. "Although we'd decided to work within the existing footprint because that was the most affordable approach, removing the pass-through completely changed everything," she says.

To infuse the room with the contemporary oceanic theme found elsewhere in the house, Jolee selected tile made with recycled shells. Pricey items such as sleek modernist cabinetry and stainless-steel appliances were made affordable with smart shopping selections. Purchasing appliances sized appropriately

ABOVE RIGHT: Pullout wire drawers maximize space and make it easy to access hard-to-reach items at the back of the slide-outs. OPPOSITE: Dishwasher drawers add a high-end touch and efficiency because smaller loads can be run on a regular basis.

Affordable Customizing

It's possible to get a high-end look on a budget, but you have to prioritize your wants and needs to determine where to save and where to splurge.

MATERIALS Choose high-quality materials that are durable and easy to clean and maintain. Perhaps more costly up front, they'll save time and money in the long run. This kitchen has quartz-surfacing countertops that never need to be refinished.

FLOORING Flooring is often one of the surfaces where the least attention is given, but it's usually worth a splurge. Mahogany plank flooring gives this kitchen a high-end look that ties in with the overall style of the rest of the house.

DETAILS Pay attention to detail. Homeowner Jolee Pink added a stainless-steel toe-kick at the base of cabinetry, which helps protect cabinets and provides a designer touch.

for the space also saved money. The best deal came when Jolee found a commercial refrigerator for $1,400 (the original price was $8,000) at a kitchen studio moving sale. Those savings made possible splurges such as the backsplash tile, dishwasher drawers, a hands-free faucet, an instant hot-water dispenser, and stereo speakers.

Now both inviting and much more functional, this kitchen serves as a how-to primer for any homeowner aspiring to make basic better without breaking the bank. "The new kitchen has changed our lifestyle," Jolee says. "And Larry was so inspired that he signed up for cooking school!"

ABOVE: Stainless steel on the appliances, faucets, hardware, and toe-kick adds luxe touches. LEFT: Frosted-glass doors contribute to the room's openness.

1. A NEW VIEW

A dual-pane window replaced an existing slider window.

2. THE BRIGHTER SIDE

Homeowner Jolee Pink selected a neutral color palette of light blue, gray, and white to make the room feel open and bright. Inexpensive undercabinet lighting adds a custom touch and illuminates counter work areas.

3. UPGRADED APPLIANCES

A commercial refrigerator was purchased for a great price during a store's moving sale. By avoiding oversize appliances and shopping the sales, the Pinks got high-end appliances on a budget.

4. ROOM FOR TWO

The Pinks brought in a contractor to remove the pass-through between the kitchen and dining room. The open space was converted into a peninsula. "Now that we have a peninsula seating area, we enjoy meals together at the counter while looking out onto the garden," Jolee says.

$ budget breakdown

- **APPLIANCES**

Dishwasher drawers	1,100
Microwave	140
Range	3,000
Range hood	501
Refrigerator	1,400

- **CABINETRY**

Cabinetry	10,937

- **PLUMBING**

Faucet	675
Instant hot water faucet	420
Sink, basket, strainer	628

- **SURFACES**

Countertop	4,350
Carpet tile	180
Tile	880

- **MISCELLANEOUS**

Cabinetry lighting	600

TOTAL	**$24,811**

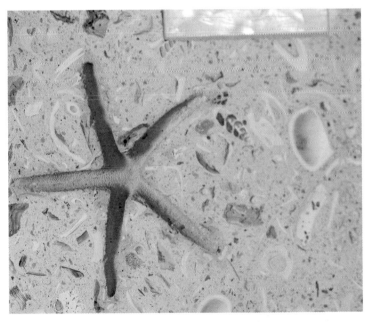

ABOVE: Embedded into the concrete backsplash are real shells and impressions of starfish made by casting actual starfish into molds, then hand-stamping them onto the tile surface. The mother-of-pearl accent tile adds a bit of shimmer and shine.

bounce-back bungalow

A to-the-studs remodel transforms a 1930s kitchen into a light-filled place for gathering.

THIS PAGE: Minimal wall cabinets and a trio of windows keep the kitchen cheerful and bright. OPPOSITE: A backsplash of glass blocks fills the kitchen with ambient light and enhances the modern-but-warm feeling.

> **" I'm an interior designer so I love to play with color. "**
>
> —HOMEOWNER ZOE PAPAS

Only a pair of bubbling optimists could have seen the potential in this downtown Burlington, Vermont, bungalow. Zoe Papas and Mark McGinley knew the home had been owned by an eccentric woman. One whiff of the home's 100-square-foot kitchen let them know that rumors were true: It had housed 30 cats. Beneath the food bowls and litter boxes, the sink, countertops, and floor were worn beyond repair. Only the range and refrigerator had been replaced within the past 75 years, and it was time for that to happen again. Bright pink walls added to the not-so-welcoming sight and frightened off any other potential buyers. But Zoe and Mark smelled opportunity amid the rubble and thought they could make a good buy.

"The home was priced to sell, and we were first-time buyers," Zoe says. "Mark, an engineer, and I knew with a little sweat equity, we could make the home— especially the kitchen—into something very special.

"I confess that on our first night in the home, I cried. The smell was overwhelming. But the next day, we started tearing out the floors and cleaning out the smell, so I knew we'd be OK."

The next step in the makeover process was to buy a kitchen design kit; the couple found one at IKEA. Armed with templates and graph paper, they toyed with the kitchen layout and concentrated on how to make the small space function best. Tearing down the wall between the eating area and work space and replacing it with a peninsula provided a straightforward way to gain more counter space and seemed like the most logical solution.

Appliance placement was the next priority for Mark and Zoe, both of whom love to cook. To optimize floor space, the couple decided to recess the

BELOW: A built-in niche keeps spices organized and close at hand. OPPOSITE: Professional-grade appliances were a top priority for homeowners and gourmet cooks Mark McGinley and Zoe Papas. "The stainless steel looks great with the concrete counters and the cabinetry hardware," Zoe says.

Room to Move

An efficient kitchen requires adequate space. Here are some basic measurements for which to strive.

CABINETS AND COUNTERTOPS Plan for 12 linear feet of cabinetry and countertops, which is considered to be a minimum. Sixteen linear feet would be better. Countertop placement should include a minimum of 15 inches of landing space near all appliances, although two appliances can share a landing space.

WALKWAYS Allow at least 36 inches for walkways; allot 42 inches if it's a traffic aisle in a work area or if multiple cooks will be crossing paths. Make sure that entry, cabinet, and appliance doors open without interference from adjacent objects and without blocking walkways.

refrigerator into the living room wall; new bookcases camouflage the bump-out. The sink and dishwasher fell into place below a window on the opposite wall, leaving the range to fit along the wall between them.

Classic white melamine cabinets with sleek stainless-steel handles fill the wall space between the appliances. The couple opted to add a large window to the sink wall and to cover the backsplash of the other wall with light-filtering glass blocks. "The only view from that wall was at the side of our neighbor's house," Zoe says. "The glass blocks let in the light." Tongue-in-groove paneling added at the ends of the cabinets reinforces the Craftsman style.

Sage green walls harken to the home's 1930s roots. "Green is my favorite color, and this shade was common in homes built during the '30s, so it was a perfect choice for the space," Zoe says.

Since completing the remodeling project, the kitchen has become one of Zoe and Mark's favorites spots in the house. Guests invariably gather around and hear a good story about the couple's optimistic approach to their kitchen's amazing transformation from a "cat house" to a charming bungalow beauty.

OPPOSITE: Enlarging the opening between the dining area and living room makes both spaces feel roomier. A shelf above the opening shows off vintage dishware.

$ budget breakdown

APPLIANCES	
Refrigerator, range, dishwasher	3,150
CABINETRY	
Cabinetry	2,400
Hardware	300
PLUMBING	
Garbage disposal	180
Sink	350
Faucet	200
COUNTERTOPS	
Custom concrete	1,600
LIGHTING	
Recessed fixtures	75
Pendants	250
WINDOWS	
Sink window	1,200
Glass block	375
PAINT	
2 gallons	60
MATERIALS	
Electrical, plumbing, construction, tile	8,740
TOTAL	**$18,880**

1. COUNTER INTUITIVE
The kitchen's U-shape work space maximizes counter space. The peninsula can also be used as a buffet.

2. LIGHT TOUCH
A 5½-foot-long glass-block backsplash provides privacy and natural light.

3. CLEAR PATH
Recessing the refrigerator into the living room wall keeps the walkway clear to the stairs.

before

Unfinished stock cabinetry looks custom with these designer tricks: a rubbed-paint finish, a mix of open shelving and solid door fronts, and hardware with a burnished patina.

splash of color

Inspired by a sailboat painting, this kitchen proves that cottage style doesn't have to mean pure white.

llen Purdum never met a color she didn't like. So when she and husband David decided to give their old kitchen the heave-ho, it seemed only natural to spin the color wheel. Though they wanted a cottage look, which traditionally means an abundance of white, color was a must for the Purdums. "To me, white and stainless are sterile," Ellen says. "I wanted lots of color, including brights." For help in transforming the kitchen, part of a Craftsman bungalow built in 1920 in a historic area between Atlanta and Stone Mountain, Georgia, the couple turned to interior designer Deborah Coleman.

The couple came to their first meeting with a list of what they wanted most: a better floor plan, more storage, a separate breakfast nook, and happy color. "Then Ellen pulled out a photo of a painting and asked, 'Is there any chance we could work with some of these colors?'" Coleman says. The sailboat painting provided the perfect way to wrap the room in cottage warmth and playfulness.

The room was gutted to remove dark, worn wood cabinetry, blue laminate counters, and a mix of appliances from the '60s, including a harvest-gold range with just one operating burner and an oven that

heated to only 200°F. Beneath the '70s gold-and-green vinyl flooring was a real find—the home's original pine. They refinished it.

"The kitchen had lots of floor space but very little work space, so reversing that balance was our first objective," Coleman says. "Also, as with many houses of this era, the kitchen wasn't designed to flow into the rest of the house or to the backyard. Instead, the kitchen door faced directly into the master bedroom." Two doors, awkwardly located in the middle of two opposite walls, moved to opposite corners of the room, where they foster better traffic flow and lead into more appropriate areas of the house—the main hallway and porch. Storage nearly quadrupled with more wall space for cabinetry. An L-shape counter configuration enables multiple cooks to work without colliding, a common occurrence when all the work space ran along one wall.

Tackling the breakfast nook was next. Because the Purdums had a tight budget, building out wasn't an option. "Luckily, there was a porch that ran along the whole back of the house and it wasn't used much," Coleman says, "so we decided to convert half of it into the breakfast room." Walls replaced the screens, and a large window and roomy window seat overlooking the garden complete the nook.

With construction finished, attention turned to finishing touches. The sailboat painting's color palette brought the kitchen to life with its earthy Mediterranean hues. "Varying the colors breaks up the severity of a kitchen and creates a bright and lively feel that's just right for a cottage kitchen," Coleman

Adding Color to a Cottage Kitchen

Break out of the neutral zone and update your light and airy cottage kitchen. Consider the following ideas.

• Paint walls and cabinets in warm hues.

• Choose burnished metal finishes for hardware and faucets.

• Add a pop of vibrant color on the back wall of open cabinetry.

• Hang a favorite piece of art or display a collection.

ABOVE LEFT: **Homeowners Ellen and David Purdum picked their kitchen's warm color palette from this painting.** ABOVE: **Multidepth cabinetry surrounds the freestanding refrigerator, creating the look of a built-in.** OPPOSITE: **Cream-color dinnerware stands out against the brightly painted beaded board. The high-arch faucet and apron-front sink are spot-on for a cottage look and also practical for cooks who have lots of fresh veggies to clean and large pots to fill.**

LEFT: Because the island is on wheels, it can go where it's needed and double as mini eating area or buffet. BELOW: Cabinetry that stops short of the 10-foot-high ceiling keeps the room from looking top-heavy. BOTTOM: Part of an unused porch is now a sunny breakfast room with a built-in window seat. Drawers underneath provide storage for linens.

says. Because natural light enters the room from only one window and the breakfast room doorway, walls were painted a soft yellow to make the space appear light and bright. Buttercream cabinets bounce the light, as does the coordinating solid-surfacing countertop. Bold orange paint brightens the back of the open wall cabinets. Other cabinets are blue with a gently distressed finish. "The distressed look was the artist's idea," Ellen says. "It keeps the darker color from looking too solid and heavy. Plus, it reminds me so much of the sea."

Unfinished cabinets and midprice appliances made it possible to splurge on two elements that deliver distinct cottage charm: the apron-front sink and the cabinetry finish. Working with a pro was also essential, Ellen says. "Deborah flagged potential problems, got us to think outside the box, and helped us play house with our imagination," she says. "Now we have a kitchen that's plenty big for the two of us to move around in, yet it still feels cozy. It's so nice to finally have appliances that work. And did I mention the color? Hands down, that's the best thing of all."

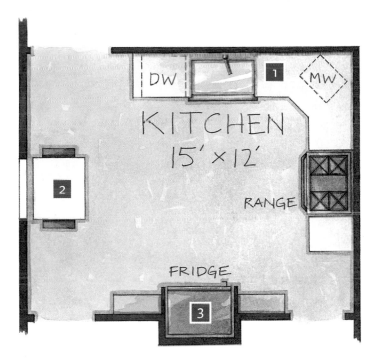

1. INCREASING STORAGE
Giving up the window over the sink made room for significantly more storage.

2. FLEX TIME
Adding wheels to the island lets it serve as a snack spot by the window or move to the center of the room for meal prep.

3. CUSTOM LOOK
To visually balance the space, the laundry room door was moved so a wall could be added. The refrigerator slides into cabinetry for a built-in look.

$ budget breakdown

- **APPLIANCES**
Dishwasher	400
Microwave	240
Range	490
Refrigerator	1,225
Vent hood	280
- **CABINETRY**
Cabinetry	15,100
- **PLUMBING**
Fixtures, including disposal	775
- **SURFACES**
Countertops	1,570
- **MISCELLANEOUS**
Custom paint	3,000
Supplies	715

TOTAL	$23,795

ABOVE: **A two-stage rubbed finish—applied to surfaces painted with a base color and two different top coats—gives the new cabinets an aged look.**

buried treasure

A Minneapolis man works past a rough
exterior to uncover a jewel of a kitchen.

THIS PHOTO: Maple cabinets with a honey stain and hand-rubbed mocha glaze warm the kitchen. OPPOSITE: A continuous grate on the range lets the cook slide pots from burner to burner with ease. The pot-filler faucet makes it simple to add water to stock pots.

Stretch a remodeling budget by doing some of the labor yourself so you can splurge on a few luxury touches.

Tile Flooring Tips

A tile floor adds an upscale look to a kitchen, but installation requires planning.

GET BELOW THE SURFACE Find out the condition of your subfloor before starting a tile project. You may need to lay a subfloor of rigid cement board to support the tile.

MEASURE UP Using a metal tape, carefully determine the room's dimensions. (BHG.com/tilecalculator can help you determine how much tile you need based on your measurements.)

MATERIALS MATTER Decide whether ceramic or natural stone tile works best for your kitchen and budget. In general, stone tile is more costly and can require more maintenance, but it gives the kitchen a timeless look.

LAY IT ON THE LINE Set out your tiles before you begin permanently affixing them. Use tile spacers, sold in varying sizes at home supply stores, to ensure consistent grout lines.

SEAL THE DEAL Natural stone tiles often are porous, so seal them before grouting. After grouting, seal the grout to avoid stains.

Tom Underwood restores homes for a living, so it came as no surprise that he wanted to do most of the work on his own kitchen. To most folks, however, the 1920s Mediterranean-style house he purchased didn't seem like promising raw material. "It was the worst house in the neighborhood," Tom says. "This one just looked like it was stuck in time."

The licensed contractor looked past the metal awnings, leaky roof, and gold shag carpeting and envisioned a kitchen with traditional charm and punches of color that would blend with the rest of the house.

Because putting an addition on the house wasn't an option, Tom decided to relocate the cooking space to an area that had previously housed cabinets and an eating area. The move created a galley style kitchen with a small adjoining dining nook—a more usable space where Tom and his partner can cook and entertain.

The rest of the house provided inspiration for the kitchen's design. For instance, the home's many arched doorways prompted Tom to create an archway between the kitchen and dining nook. "I always try to match what's there," he says. "You'd never know it wasn't there originally."

Tom's faith in the kitchen's potential was rewarded when he uncovered relatively rare 1-inch maple flooring

ABOVE: **Natural-hue domino tiles add interest to the floor's oversize tiles, all which cover a hidden luxury: an in-floor heating system.** OPPOSITE: **Tom Underwood found his stainless-steel appliances on sale. Placing the microwave/ convection oven directly above the cooktop saved space.**

THIS PHOTO: An archway provides a glimpse into the cozy dining nook. Tom purchased the red-glass Italian light fixture specifically for the eating area.
OPPOSITE: Building the dining table against the wall makes the most of the nook. Natural light from an east-facing window brightens the space.

budget breakdown

APPLIANCES	
Cooktop	300
Dishwasher	650
Microwave	600
Refrigerator	2,000
Wall oven	1,200
WALLS AND WORK SURFACES	
Granite countertops	3,000
Paint	20
Tile	300
LIGHTS AND ELECTRICAL	
Recessed lights	150
Ceiling speakers	200
Volume controls	20
CABINETRY	
Cabinetry	8,000
Stainless-steel pulls	100
SINK AREA	
Faucet	325
Garbage disposal	65
Sink	600
TOTAL	**$17,530**

in the dining nook. Although it was mostly intact, the few areas that did need to be replaced required costly custom-milled boards. Luckily, Tom was able to save money on other parts of the kitchen, most notably by doing much of the work himself. He estimates his labor saved him more than $30,000.

The tile work for the kitchen floor was one of his bigger projects. He chose 12×12-inch slate tiles in a warm shade of brown. "I like working with natural stone," he says. "It's timeless, and it's always in style." To break up the pattern of large tiles, he added a band of small domino-style tiles.

For cabinetry, Tom shopped at a home center. He chose high-end cabinets, some with glass fronts to showcase china and stemware. Dimmer switches control most of the lighting. "It creates nice mood lighting," he says. "Nothing blinds you."

Tom remodeled several other homes prior to tackling his own, but he's most proud of this kitchen. "You look at its quality," he says, "and you know it's going to be here a long time."

1. SUNNY SPOT
The east-facing window makes the nook a pleasant place to start the day with a cup of coffee.

2. COOKING EASE
An extra-deep sink and pullout faucet inspire serious cooking.

3. SMOOTH FLOW
The long, narrow space lends itself well to a galley-style kitchen arrangement.

culinary delights

5

Some kitchens just make a person smile. It might be because of the room's daring color, such as a bright lime backsplash. Perhaps it's a basic piece of pegboard with pans hanging on it, an homage to legendary cook Julia Child. Or maybe it's the unexpected surprises—a movable island that can be a wherever-needed buffet, a hallway closet retrofitted into a pantry, or the amazing gourmet features packed into a not-so-big cooking zone.

Take a look around your kitchen to see where it could use a little boost. Is the backsplash a blank slate? Ceramic or glass tile will splash it with color; tin or metal will lend texture and shine. Maybe it's time to indulge your passions by building in cubbies to store wine bottles or mounting a little television below a cabinet. Lifting the mood can even be as simple as hanging a new pendant, removing doors from a few cabinets and letting dishes star, or putting the orange mixer you love out on the countertop. A kitchen isn't all work and no play. So by all means, play.

small but mighty

This storage-savvy New York kitchen offers all the amenities of a room twice its size.

THIS PHOTO: Marilyn and Len Feingold's kitchen, which now opens to the dining area, is a storage workhorse. Cubbies in the peninsula were built to store wine bottles. OPPOSITE: Not an inch of space was wasted. A spice rack above the range hood makes use of a shallow area.

Space is always at a premium in a kitchen. In Marilyn and Len Feingold's Manhattan apartment, however, it took especially careful planning to maximize storage and function. The result: a compact, contemporary kitchen full of great solutions and amenities.

The centerpiece is a storage-packed peninsula. Deep drawers on both sides accommodate large cookware. A multitude of drawers and pullouts keep utensils and pantry items organized. Granite with red veining tops the peninsula.

The stunning colors of the countertop make the kitchen a showstopper. "Marilyn had this vision," kitchen designer James Jones says. "I just helped guide her along the way."

Her inspiration? "I wanted a pomegranate kitchen," Marilyn says. "Pomegranates symbolize mitzvahs, or good deeds. What else could you want for your home?" The red in the granite complements the red soffit and the many pomegranate accents throughout the room.

BELOW: **Next to the sink and sleek faucet is a smaller faucet that provides hot water instantly. It's a great amenity for preparing a cup of tea.** BELOW RIGHT: **The microwave oven is integrated into the backsplash, where soft green glass tiles reflect natural light. Wavy grates on the range add a fun element.**

The kitchen is much more than aesthetically pleasing. It's also an efficient, space-savvy workplace. To the right of the range, the microwave is recessed into the wall, leaving counter space open for prep work. Below the microwave, and disguised with cabinetry panels, is a warming drawer.

Other appliances, such as the dishwasher and refrigerator, have the same cabinetry panels and sleek aluminum hardware, which give the space a seamless modern look. Frosted-glass panels on wall cabinets offer a visual break and infuse the space with contemporary sophistication.

RIGHT: **Deep drawers rather than cabinets make it easy to access items. Cubbies for wine bottles could also be used for storing cooking gadgets in slim bins.** BELOW: **A warming drawer keeps meals perfectly plated.** BELOW RIGHT: **Wall-mounted rails that accommodate shelves and towel bars offer flexible storage options. The shelves can slide from side to side or be removed depending on storage needs.**

deco perfecto

Red appliances, white cabinets, and old blueprints create an accurate copy of a home's 1930s kitchen.

A love of Art Deco style inspired Kathleen and Paxton Mendelssohn to restore the kitchen of their 1930s home to its former glory. Without changing the room's size, the couple created a happy little hub that's now the pride of their St. Petersburg home.

The Mendelssohns' first order of business was to undo a 1950s redo that was out of sync with both the era of the home and modern living. They tapped designer Dorothy Mainello, a member of the National Kitchen & Bath Association (NKBA), to help them take the design back to the 1930s but push the conveniences into the present.

Having the original blueprints was a big ace in putting the kitchen back together after gutting it. Those blueprints guided the layout, which features a simple triangular work zone. Mainello also copied the original cabinetry as closely as possible, in both style and configuration. While

LEFT: A wooden shelf above the reproduction range reminds one of the homeowners of the house he grew up in. OPPOSITE: The peninsula eating area gives this retro kitchen a playful diner feel.

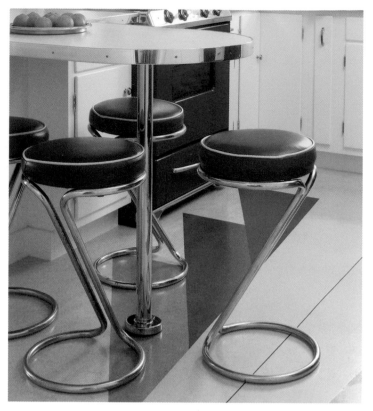

RIGHT: The countertop to the right of the refrigerator works as a handy desk and landing spot for items headed in and out of the microwave oven, which is housed in the cabinets above. OPPOSITE TOP, LEFT: The range's chrome detailing, which incorporates an analog clock, conveys the industrial side of Art Deco style. OPPOSITE TOP, RIGHT: The arrow pattern in the linoleum floor is typical of Deco's geometric bent. OPPOSITE BOTTOM, LEFT: This restored 1930s Stromberg-Carlson phone was once the height of sophistication. OPPOSITE BOTTOM, RIGHT: The nickel-stamped wall plate is a reproduction of a Deco design. The chrome vase is a 1930s piece.

the white-painted cabinets say classic kitchen, the candy red appliances that team with them reflect the boldness of Art Deco hues. The refrigerator, range, and range hood are reproductions that meld the function of today's appliances with the character of vintage ones.

Appliances aside, it's the attention to detail that really enhances the kitchen's period appeal. No matter how small the design element, the couple's goal was to be period faithful. A case in point is the aluminum trim between the countertop and wall. In the past—in the absence of a tile backsplash—the trim kept food crumbs and liquids from falling behind cabinets. Even the accessories are authentic. Chrome Z stools, re-covered in red, are 1930s models by famed industrial designer Gilbert Rohde. Salt-and-pepper shakers on a shelf above the range belonged to Paxton's grandmother.

There is one nonperiod concession to convenience. Although linoleum was the top 1930s counter surface, Paxton wanted something more knife-friendly. A linoleum-look laminate edged with polished aluminum fills the bill. In a room that brims with so many engaging Art Deco elements, no one will even have time to spot the substitution.

FAITHFUL FOOTPRINT

The original blueprints guided the configuration of this period-inspired kitchen. The refrigerator, for example, occupies the same spot once held by the original icebox. Contained behind the peninsula, the work zone is an efficient triangle with counter space on all sides of the appliances and sink. A modern problem—where to put the microwave—was solved simply. The microwave is out of sight in a cabinet by the refrigerator.

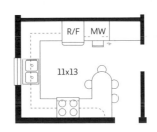

before

bright spot

For such a tiny space, this kitchen packs a lot in—and also packs a lot of punch. Its lively tile sets a fresh, fun tone.

before

OPPOSITE: With one of the short walls removed, this kitchen is more accessible and seems larger. Glass-front cabinets also add a sense of spaciousness. The insides of the cabinets are painted blue—a simple touch that makes displayed dishes stand out. ABOVE: Compact appliances, including a 24-inch-wide range, are key to the room's functionality. The cabinet in the remaining short wall serves as a pantry.

When work began to take photography team Kim Cornelison and Alfie Ferreyra to Minneapolis for frequent assignments, the couple began looking for a place to put down roots in the city they loved. They purchased a 750-square-foot place in a 1920s apartment building being converted to condos. The small, cozy home had a lot going for it. "We loved the natural light and its urban location," Kim says. The couple also appreciated the hardwood floors and some of the original kitchen cabinetry. That's not to say the kitchen didn't have shortcomings: Its layout was nearly unworkable, it lacked storage, and the old cabinetry was too shallow and too short.

To start overhauling their condo and set their design course in motion, Kim and Alfie assembled an "inspiration board" that included paint, fabric, and tiles. They then consulted with friend and designer David Anger, who helped them pull together their country-in-the-city look.

Alfie focused his attention on designing the kitchen and making sense of its 11×7-foot layout. He pulled up vinyl flooring and removed one short wall to make the room more accessible.

Upper cabinets were saved and rehung higher on the wall. After stripping off the layers of old paint, the cabinets revealed a welcome surprise: original glass panels. Lower cabinets got the heave-ho to make room for a suite of small-scale appliances, which are integrated into new custom cabinets.

The skinny appliances are the genius behind the kitchen's full-size function. The range, with burners spanning the top of the unit, looks hunkier than its 24-inch width. Cabinetry panels conceal a compact refrigerator to the right of it and a whisper-quiet 18-inch-wide dishwasher in the area with the glass-front cabinets.

Function isn't the end-all of this little gem of a room, though. The tile that covers backsplashes and countertops brings playful pattern and fresh color to the space. It also set the tone for other rooms. "All the colors in the condo relate back to the yellow, green, and blue found in the kitchen tile," Anger says.

With Anger's help, the couple finished layering the small space with easy-to-change accessories that continue the color story. "Natural flooring, vintage touches, and random artifacts bring it to life," Anger says.

RIGHT: **The dining room carries through the colors in the kitchen, helping the two small spaces seem more cohesive. An inexpensive Colonial chandelier gets a modern touch with unexpected round bulbs.** OPPOSITE LEFT: **A framed pegboard provides practical storage for pans, towels, and small cooking utensils. It's also a fun touch: The pegboard was inspired by one that hung in the kitchen of legendary cook Julia Child.** OPPOSITE RIGHT: **Apron-front styling makes the sink look more substantial.**

Take-Home Tip
A round table with a pedestal base functions best in a small space. It allows more legroom and is visually light.

A wine refrigerator and a television mounted under a corner cabinet are among the little luxuries tucked into this remodeled kitchen.

maximized modern

Eye-catching color and a movable island make the most of a midcentury kitchen.

Heralded as a model of modern living when developed in the late 1950s, Toronto's Don Mills neighborhood boasts contemporary ranch homes characterized by simple materials, open spaces, and integration with nature.

Sandra and Walter Cifersons fell in love with one of those homes. However, they were less fond of its original kitchen, which featured pink plastic doors, dated laminate countertops, an awkward U-shape layout, and walls that closed off the space from living and dining areas. "It was modern for the time, with a European influence, but hadn't aged well," says Walter, an architectural designer.

The couple lived with the kitchen for 15 years before starting a long-awaited renovation. "Our goal was a space that was open, flexible, and respectful of the style of the house," Walter says. "Form and function in equal proportions."

Because the home is near a ravine, adding on was out. "We knew our only option was to make the existing space work smarter," says Jan Regis, a certified master kitchen and bath designer (CMKBD) and member of the National Kitchen & Bath Association (NKBA). Regis and architect Howard Rideout worked with the couple.

Taking down the walls adjoining the living and dining areas instantly made the kitchen seem larger. The openness also made the kitchen look more in sync with the rest of the home; the living room features a cathedral ceiling and floor-to-ceiling fireplace.

The design team updated the floor plan to add cabinets and counter space on the remaining walls. That gave the couple the storage and work space they craved. The flexibility Walter wanted comes through in the center island. Although it looks like a permanent fixture, it's movable. "The island was Walter's idea," Regis says. "It works for prep as well as entertaining, and can be moved in different formations for added buffet or work space—or even out of the way altogether."

The island is topped with quartz-surfacing, as are the base cabinets on the cooktop wall. The sink-wall cabinetry features a stainless-steel countertop with a water-catching lip. Compact built-in appliances—including an 18-inch-wide dishwasher by the sink—help the modest-size space live large.

A new picture window on the sink wall lets in natural light and frames views of the ravine below. It was the ravine that inspired the home's most distinctive feature—a backsplash back-painted in what Regis calls wasabi green. "The couple wanted a strong accent color, and were inspired by the variations of green in the woods nearby," Regis says. "It's eye-catching, but not overpowering, and adds punch to the more neutral maple-laminate cabinets."

The green reflects not only the view outside, but also the couple's commitment to using natural building products, including sustainable bamboo on the floor. And it makes them smile. "The back-painted glass is still as fresh and fun as the first day we installed it," Walter says.

ABOVE: A stainless-steel countertop with an integral sink makes a practical prep and cleanup area. FAR LEFT: A two-level movable island holds the microwave and a warming drawer. LEFT: Inches count in a small kitchen. A slim pullout keeps spices close to the cooktop and oven. OPPOSITE: The back-painted glass backsplash reflects light from the window and provides a colorful counterpoint to maple cabinets and bamboo flooring. Slim rod-style handles on the cabinets elongate the room.

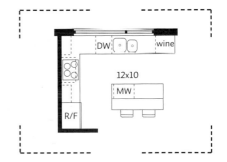

taking stock

With its first new look in decades, this kitchen scores off the charts. The key? A few smart shifts, including turning a hallway closet into a walk-in pantry for loading up on supplies.

It was love at first sight for Rebecca and Jason Barnes. "We'd found a house with its absolute original kitchen, complete with yellow and black-accented tile and vintage sink and fixtures," says Rebecca, a Dallas architect who's now a stay-at-home mom. Soon, reality set in. With no dishwasher and only one short wall of cabinets, the 8×11-foot space wasn't working.

The couple's challenge was to give the kitchen a classic look but add modern conveniences. Rebecca's to-do list included moving a water heater, adding storage, improving traffic flow, and updating the room's lighting and appliances.

The solution came by thinking through every move. Rebecca moved a door to make room for more cabinets and counters. She relocated the water heater to a closet on the back porch, freeing up room next to the new range. And she even eked out space for a

ABOVE LEFT: Hardware gives the cabinetry an authentic look. The original hinges were surface mounts, so homeowners Rebecca and Jason Barnes kept the same idea. "It showcases the hardware well," Rebecca says. LEFT: For a cheap take on oxidized metal, Jason painted tin tiles with muriatic acid from a home center, then sealed and waxed the tiles before adhering them to the wall with adhesive and adding furniture tacks. (Wearing protective clothing, glasses, gloves, and a mask are essential for such a project.) OPPOSITE: A new window with a large fixed pane and twin hinged side panels allows more light into the once-dreary kitchen.

walk-in pantry—a practical luxury for any kitchen. The pantry came by looking beyond the kitchen's four walls. It's actually a closet under a stairwell adjacent to the kitchen. Cooking supplies, small appliances, and linens are organized on shelves inside the pantry.

Although the sleek new stainless-steel appliances speak to modern times, Rebecca took care to retain the kitchen's vintage charm. A cabinetmaker family member helped build old-style cabinets (and keep costs down). Painted a greenish-gray, the cabinets prove that a small kitchen doesn't have to have light-color cabinetry to visually expand it. "We just added more lighting options so it wouldn't be too dark," Rebecca says. In fact, she says a pale palette "would have been too much of a jolt" for the room.

She also resisted the temptation to add trendy countertops. "My husband and I talked about having granite, stainless-steel, or concrete counters, but we decided they'd look and feel too cold in here," Rebecca says. For a warmer, lighter look, they went with maple butcher block. In a large kitchen, that might have been a splurge, "but not in this case, since the space was so small," Rebecca says.

Today, the kitchen is as Rebecca imagined it could be—warm and inviting, despite its small size. "People still stand in here like sardines, but it feels much more open now," she says.

ABOVE: A formerly messy closet under a stairwell across from the kitchen is now a tidy and well-lit pantry for canned goods, small appliances, and kitchen linens. Above the built-ins, shelves on brackets were sized to fit the slanted wall, capitalizing on storage space. LEFT: A custom-built wall unit that resembles the cabinetry is a handy drop-off spot for keys, notes, and bills. Bonus: It frees up counter space. OPPOSITE: An arched doorway replaced a swinging door to the dining room. Removing layers of linoleum and laying matching oak flooring eased the transition between rooms. Removing the door from one of the upper cabinets creates display space and a handy place for cookbooks.

kitchen workbook

Planning a kitchen is like being in school—you have to do the homework. Choosing cabinetry, countertops, tile, and other elements can be overwhelming. Do you want natural wood or painted cabinets? Should you go with a stainless-steel sink or acrylic? Have you decided on laminate countertops, or will you splurge for granite? This guide will lead you through the decision-making process.

As you study up on the options, you'll need to do some math. Once you determine your budget, consider dividing it according to these percentages recommended by kitchen experts: 40 percent for cabinetry, 15 percent for countertops, 15 percent for appliances, 5 percent for flooring, 2 percent for fixtures, and 22 percent for "other." The bottom line? A little preplanning and diligence will move you one step closer to acing your kitchen renovation project.

cabinets

No other single element has the transforming power of cabinetry. Natural or stained cabinets add richness, while painted or glazed ones lend character and color. Clear- or frosted-glass doors can help visually stretch a small space. After you decide on a style, take inventory of your storage needs to make sure your cabinets will be functional, not just pretty.

Your choices

STOCK Available either ready-to-assemble (RTA) or ready-to-install, stock cabinetry ranges from 6 to 42 inches wide, in 3-inch increments. Depths tend to be the standard 12 inches for wall cabinets and 24 inches for base cabinets. Quality ranges widely in this category, which is the least-expensive option. Steer clear of half-inch particleboard with a plastic veneer.

SEMICUSTOM This is by far the largest market for kitchen cabinetry. Semicustom cabinetry, which is factory-made, comes in standard sizes but offers more options in finishes, features, and materials. Semicustom is an economical choice if you want better quality and more options than stock cabinetry, but don't want the added expense of custom cabinets. Allow several weeks—or even a few months—of lead time for orders.

CUSTOM Custom cabinetry is designed, built, and installed to fit a unique space. The layout is usually determined with the assistance of a professional kitchen designer. Exotic materials, ornate detailing, and radically different styles will increase the cost of custom cabinetry but create a one-of-a-kind kitchen.

Note: When shopping for cabinets, keep in mind that most cabinet boxes are now made using engineered wood products such as medium-density fiberboard (MDF), particleboard, or plywood. These products are veneered or laminated. Engineered wood cabinets are less likely than solid-wood cabinets to expand or contract over time. For a more contemporary look, metal cabinetry is also available.

Quality Indicators

Buying the cheapest cabinetry available is rarely the best choice. When comparing cabinets, ask about construction details and look for these signs of lasting quality.

- Drawers should have solid-wood or plywood sides with rabbeted, doweled, or dovetailed joints.

- Self-closing drawers and tray glides should be able to bear 75–100 pounds each. Ball bearings are best.

- Adjustable shelves in wall cabinets allow for greater storage flexibility.

- Pullout trays in lower cabinetry are more efficient than fixed shelves.

Natural wood: Consider the grain

Wood grain makes as much of a statement as color. Notice the differences.

MAPLE

BIRCH

CHERRY

HICKORY

OAK

Door design: Choose your style

Cabinetry doors can dominate the look of a room. Consider which door shape, type of insert, and frame style suits your space before placing a cabinetry order.

Shapes

SQUARE

ARCH

CATHEDRAL

SLAB

Inserts

RAISED PANEL

RECESSED PANEL

BEADED BOARD

DECORATIVE MOLDING

Glossary

FULL OVERLAY
Doors cover the face frame—or the entire box front on frameless cabinets—leaving only a sliver of space between doors and drawers. This creates a modern, clean look.

PARTIAL OVERLAY
Doors cover the face frame by half an inch, and the frame shows all the way around the door. This traditional style is the easiest to construct and the most affordable option.

FULL-INSET
Doors and drawers fit flush with the face frame. Because this technique requires patience and precision, it's typically only available in custom cabinetry.

countertops

A visual partner to your cabinets, countertops should be stylish yet sensible. After all, this hardworking surface is the one you touch most. You don't have to choose one perfect surface—using more than one is fun and functional. Factor in your budget, favorite colors, and textures, but also consider durability, maintenance, and repairability.

Your choices

CERAMIC TILE This heat-resistant surface comes in an abundance of shapes, colors, and sizes. It's easy to clean, but grout may discolor. Uneven surfaces can chip, but the tiles can be replaced. For countertops, hard, nonporous, glazed vitreous tiles tend to be the best option.

CONCRETE Available in almost any color, concrete has the ability to take on nearly any look you want. Marbles, mirror pieces, or other items can be mixed with it for a special effect. Concrete can't handle high heat, and must be sealed regularly.

GRANITE Synonymous with luxury, granite is durable, sleek, and impervious to heat. Some varieties need sealing against stains. Granite is heavy, ranging from ¾ inch to 1½ inches thick; an optional honed surface yields a nongloss finish. If you don't mind grout lines, granite tiles can cost half as much as slabs.

LAMINATE With hundreds of patterns, colors, and textures—some that mimic the look of stone, metal, or wood—laminate has made a comeback. In addition to being affordable, it's easy to install and easy to clean, but can be scorched.

LAMINATED MAPLE This hardwood glued together in a butcher-block pattern tends to be better for baking areas and island tops than countertops. Seal with mineral oil every four to eight weeks. Hot pans can scorch it, but sanding fixes minor damage.

MARBLE AND LIMESTONE Both of these natural stones are classic and luxurious. They're softer than granite and more porous. They can be scratched or stained, and gain a patina over time. (See more details and photos, *opposite page*.)

QUARTZ-SURFACING A blend of mostly quartz with resins and pigments, this surface is known for intense hues and consistent pattern not found in natural stone. Quartz-surfacing is nonporous and heat- and scratch-resistant. It's priced similar to natural stone but has the advantage of not needing to be sealed.

SOAPSTONE This vintage favorite is heat-resistant but stains easily. It's more likely to chip or crack than granite. An engineered version called Fireslate offers similar looks with better performance properties. (See more details and photo, *opposite page*.)

SOLID-SURFACING Color and pattern is a signature of solid-surfacing, which is made of synthetic resins. The ¼- to 1½-inch-thick material is nonporous, resists scorching, and is easy to clean and repair. The sink can be integrated with the countertop for a seamless look. Corian falls in this category.

STAINLESS STEEL This material is known for its contemporary appeal. Stainless steel is sanitary and resists stains and scorches. Scratches and fingerprints show until a patina develops. Countertops must be custom-fabricated.

WOOD Durable wood species such as mahogany, maple, and walnut can be sealed with oil to create a food-safe surface. The overall look of wood countertops is warm and rich.

Countertop Favorites by Function Area

No one countertop material suits all kitchen functions. Mixing materials creates a distinctive look and allocates the most practical surface to each task.

SALAD OR VEGETABLE PREP Laminated butcher block is forgiving of small cuts.

NEAR THE STOVE Heat-resistant granite, quartz-surfacing, and ceramic tile won't scorch. Consider using a trivet to avoid thermoshock.

AROUND THE SINK Stainless steel, quartz-surfacing, and solid-surfacing take top honors in this area because they're moisture-resistant and durable.

BAKING AREA Marble's always-cool surface is ideal for rolling out dough.

Stone: Compare and contrast

Stone is a popular choice for countertops. As these samples show, the options go beyond granite. Explore the many colors and patterns of lesser-known stones.

SOAPSTONE
Silky to the touch, this stone is durable and can handle high heat. Over time it will age, but oiling it will maintain the dark color.
$100-$130
per square foot

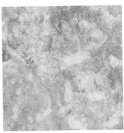

TRAVERTINE
This creamy, earth hue stone has been used in construction for thousands of years. Travertine needs to be sealed regularly.
$60-$100
per square foot

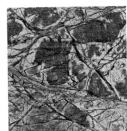

MARBLE
Synonymous with luxury and beauty, marble is also a high-maintenance and costly stone. It must be sealed to block stains.
$70-$150
per square foot

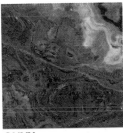

ONYX
A form of limestone, onyx looks translucent. Because it is soft and slightly brittle, it cannot endure a lot of wear and tear.
$125-$150
per square foot

LIMESTONE
Its gentle hues and wavy appearance make it silky-smooth on countertops. It comes in a variety of colors and must be sealed.
$70-$100
per square foot

SLATE
Found mostly in a matte finish, this stone resists stains and needs little maintenance. You can find slate in blue, gray, green, and brown.
Price varies greatly by region

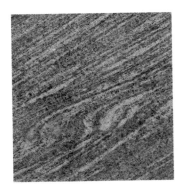

What does it mean when the granite salesperson talks about movement?

Different rates of heating and pressure develop the stone's pattern. Pieces that look like they have something flowing through them are considered to have movement. Granite styles with more movement tend to be more expensive.

Five Questions to Ask Yourself About Counters

1. WHAT'S MY BUDGET?
Knowing your limitations will put you on the right path. Remember, even prices of granite can vary drastically. There are often great cost-saving alternatives to popular pricey items if you're willing to search them out.

2. WHAT DO I LIKE AND DISLIKE ABOUT MY CURRENT COUNTERTOPS?
By analyzing your existing surface, you can get on track when it comes to your needs for the new countertops.

3. HOW MUCH MAINTENANCE DO I WANT TO UNDERTAKE AFTER THEY'RE INSTALLED?
Some countertop surfaces may require continuous attention—resealing the grout between ceramic tiles or sealing porous stones such as limestone. Others, such as solid-surfacing, are durable without any fuss.

4. HOW WILL I USE MY COUNTERTOP?
The way you cook in your kitchen narrows your choices. If you plan to set hot pots directly onto your counter, be sure the surface can handle it. The same is true for cutting, as well as frequent spills.

5. DO I EXPECT MY SURFACES TO MAINTAIN A BRAND NEW APPEARANCE?
Some of the hottest countertop and backsplash materials—stainless steel, copper, soapstone, and wood—wear with time. If you don't like the aged look, choose something else.

Glossary

BACKSPLASH
Protection of the wall at the back edge of the countertop. Designed to seal the counter and protect the wall from spills and damage. Can be integral to the counter or applied directly to the wall.

EDGE TREATMENT
Special shaping or materials applied to the front edge of a countertop, usually to provide a rounded contour or to hide the exposed edge of the substrate.

SUBSTRATE
The structural material, often either particleboard or plywood, to which a finished surface material, such as tile or laminate, is applied for a finished countertop.

backsplashes

The wall space between countertops and upper cabinets (and behind the range) is a perfect place to add pizzazz. A tiled backsplash, whether boldly colored or blended with the countertops, finishes a kitchen off in style and gives a small space personality. Because you're not covering entire walls, a tiled backsplash can be an affordable upgrade.

Your choices

CERAMIC AND PORCELAIN The wide array of colors, shapes, and sizes is a hallmark of ceramic and porcelain tiles. The finish can be matte or glossy, giving you some flexibility in how much the backsplash stands out. Ceramic and porcelain are heat-resistant and easy to clean, although grout may discolor. Price range: $2 per square foot, uninstalled, for basic ceramic tile; $8–$30 for upscale designs. Handpainted tile can cost $50 or more per piece.

GLASS Surprisingly strong, glass tiles boast great color depth. They have a shimmering, liquid-look surface that reacts to light in a distinctive way. Glass tiles come in many colors, finish styles, sizes, and shapes, allowing one-of-a-kind looks. Although glass tends to be the priciest tile surface, it's not necessarily a huge splurge when used for a backsplash since you're not covering entire walls, like may be done in a bathroom. Price range: Starting at $15–$20 per square foot.

METAL Striking and practical, metal instantly brightens a kitchen. A stainless-steel backsplash offers an industrial look that coordinates with today's popular appliance and faucet finishes. Warm metal tiles such as copper, bronze, and pewter contribute old-world charm. Metal is impervious to stains and heat, but scratches easily—not a major concern when used on a backsplash. Getting a metallic look doesn't require actual metal. While some tiles are the real deal, others earn the look from a glazed metal finish. If an all-metal backsplash is too much, use accent tiles to embellish a design of ceramic or stone tile. Price range: As low as 50 cents each for 1×1-inch metallic accent pieces and up to $100 each for handcrafted metal tiles.

STONE Natural stone tile such as granite, marble, and limestone is synonymous with luxury and offers a sense of permanence. Stone is porous and can stain, so make sure tiles are properly sealed. Price range: $4–$15 per square foot, uninstalled. Rarer stones can cost $40–$60 per square foot.

Grout Good to Know

Choosing grout can be as important as selecting tile. You can achieve different effects depending upon the color you choose.

BLEND IN Select a grout color that closely matches the color of the tile to create a uniform look.

HIDE GRIME Dark-color grout hides dirt better than light-color grout, which can be difficult to clean.

STAND OUT To make tiles stand out, choose a grout color that contrasts with the tile, such as white grout against blue tiles. The contrast will emphasize the shape of the tile, drawing attention to it

Glossary

BACKSPLASH
Protection of the wall at the back edge of the countertop; designed to seal the counter and protect the wall from spills and damage. Can be integral to the countertop or applied directly to the wall.

LISTELLOS
Decorative pieces usually installed as accent pieces or as a transition from one material to the next. Commonly referred to as border tiles. Can be expensive.

MOSAIC TILES
Small tiles generally ranging from ½x½ inch to 2x2 inches; 1-inch-square tiles are most common. Tend to be available in sheets backed with netting that makes installation easier.

SUBWAY TILES
Rectangular tiles (often 4x6 inches); typically white or light colored.

sinks and faucets

A kitchen workhorse during meal preparation and cleanup, your sink must star in function and durability. With today's wealth of styles and materials, the sink also plays a strong supporting role in your kitchen's design. To reduce installation costs, plan the location of the sink (the standard size is 22×30 inches) to take advantage of existing plumbing lines. Then outfit your sink with a faucet that also marries function and looks.

Your choices

Sink materials

ACRYLIC, COMPOSITE, AND SOLID-SURFACING All of these materials have a stone look with less weight and offer seamless installation. A molded-through color hides chips and scratches.

ENAMELED STEEL AND CAST IRON Both finishes are available in many colors. Enameled steel may chip; enameled cast iron is heavy but more durable.

STAINLESS STEEL This is today's most popular sink material and a natural complement to stainless-steel appliances. Stainless steel is affordable, easy to clean, and durable (though it scratches). Consider the steel's thickness—the "gauge"—when shopping. The lower the number, the thicker and more durable the stainless steel. An 18-gauge sink is considered a good thickness. Brushed and satin finishes wear better and consequently look better longer.

STONE Stone options include slate, soapstone, concrete, fireclay, and one-piece granite. The look is chic and organic. Stone sinks need to be sealed and are unforgiving to dropped dishes. They also tend to be costly to buy and install.

Faucet considerations

FIT Your sink (and the holes in its deck) will determine the type of faucet you can get. Will two handles fit, or would one be better? Is there room for a sprayer and/or soap dispenser? Consider the sink's size, too. Is your sink so large that only a pullout faucet will deliver water to all corners of the basin?

STYLE Obviously, you want the faucet to complement the overall look of the room—be it traditional or contemporary. But the faucet should also be functional. A single-handle faucet offers ease in regulating water temperature and mixing cold and hot. Ergonomic features include lever or wrist-blade handles, pull-down sprayers, left- or right-side single-lever mounts, and adjustable-height spouts.

FINISHES Durable polished chrome is still the most popular finish, but matte and brushed metals are coming on strong—particularly chrome and nickel to complement stainless-steel appliances. Matte and brushed bronze, brass, and copper finishes flatter old-world decor. Polymer coatings make finishes with color easier to care for, and tarnish-proof coatings are a worthwhile upgrade.

Glossary

BRIDGE FAUCET
Traditional style; deck- or wall-mount, with handles and spout linked by an exposed tube.

CARTRIDGE
Controls water flow on a faucet.

COUNTERTOP CUTOUT
An opening in the countertop that accepts and sometimes supports the sink.

DROP-IN/SELF-RIMMING SINK
Has a raised rim or lip that rests on the countertop. Lip helps support the sink.

FARMHOUSE SINK
Also called apron-front sink. Single, large rectangular bowl with an exposed apron front.

GOOSENECK OR HIGH-ARC FAUCET
Tall, arched spout that makes it easy to fill large or deep pots and tall vases.

POT-FILLER FAUCET
Wall spigot that delivers cold water only. Mounted near the range or over the cooktop for cooking convenience.

PULLOUT FAUCET
Two-piece spout functioning as both a faucet and a pullout sprayer.

SINGLE-HOLE FAUCET
Also called post-mount faucet. One hole pierces the sink deck or countertop.

UNDERMOUNT SINK
Also called rimless. Sink is mounted below the countertop so no rim or lip shows.

floors

A kitchen floor gets heavy traffic, so it should be tough and easy to maintain. As a large surface, flooring also makes a decorative impact, even in a small kitchen. Consider your lifestyle and the style of your home to choose a durable and good-looking floor that suits both.

Your choices

BAMBOO A more quickly renewable resource than wood, durable (and once exotic) bamboo has become mainstream. It's available in different patterns and plank sizes. Sunlight may fade or darken bamboo. Price range: $4–$8 per square foot, installed.

CERAMIC/PORCELAIN Strength and durability, coupled with countless colors, textures, and designs, are the hallmarks of these tiles. Ceramic and porcelain are easy to clean (though grout lines can be difficult), but are cold and hard on feet and dropped dishes. Porcelain tiles are typically more durable. Not all ceramic and porcelain tiles are rated for floor use. Price range: $8–$50 per square foot, installed.

CORK Bark from cork oak trees is used for this durable "green" flooring that resists moisture and germs. Cork is cushiony, quiet, and comfortable. Polyurethane finishes typically last up to seven years before the cork needs to be refinished. Acrylic and wax finishes are not as long-lasting. Price range: $4–$9 per square foot, installed.

LAMINATE A tougher version of the plastic laminate used for countertops, laminate flooring can imitate wood, stone, or ceramic tile, and offers unusual patterns and designs. Durability is good (though on low-quality laminate the top layer may peel from the core), and maintenance duties are light. Planks, strips, and squares glue or click together, often as a floating floor. Price range: $3–$10 per square foot, installed.

LINOLEUM Rich colors and patterns distinguish linoleum, which is made from natural raw materials. Available in sheets or tiles, linoleum repels dirt and resists bacteria. Solid colors and flecks are embedded throughout, rather than imprinted on the surface. It's more durable than vinyl, but it should be resealed annually and may scuff. Price range: $5–$9 per square foot, installed.

STONE Limestone, marble, granite, travertine, and slate make luxurious and extremely durable floors, but are unforgiving on feet and dropped items. Sweep them daily to minimize abrasions, and seal them every one to two years to guard against stains. Polished surfaces can be slippery when wet; honed tiles solve this problem. Price range: $8–$50 per square foot, installed.

VINYL Dramatic visuals—stone, tile, wood, sisal, and more—combine with comfort and easy maintenance in today's vinyl offerings. A dropped glass may bounce instead of break, and spills wipe up easily. Vinyl is less expensive than other flooring choices, but it's also difficult to repair. Look for it in tiles (including inexpensive self-adhesive squares for quick DIY updates) or sheets; 12-foot-wide rolls help avoid seams. Price range: $1–$7 per square foot, installed.

WOOD If you clean up spills quickly, acrylic and urethane finishes make wood practical for kitchens. Milled solid wood can be refinished multiple times. Engineered wood is cross-laminated to resist warping, but its top hardwood layer may be refinished just once or twice. It shrinks and expands less than solid wood and takes less time to install. Both types come in strips, planks, and parquet squares. Price range: $4–$20 per square foot, installed.

Glossary

FLOATING FLOOR
Tongue-and-groove laminate or engineered-wood sections connected to each other but not fixed to the floor beneath.

INLAID VINYL
Colored vinyl chips create heat-fused patterns and provide color throughout the entire thickness, not just on the surface.

PLANK FLOORING
Boards wider than 3 inches.

RESILIENT
Vinyl, linoleum, cork, and rubber tiles and sheets cushioned for comfort and flexibility.

STRIP FLOORING
Boards less than 3 inches wide.

WEAR LAYER
Visible surface of synthetic coating factory-applied to resilient flooring.

lighting

Choosing lighting for your kitchen is like planning a full-course meal. Just as your dinner improves with a variety of dishes, your kitchen benefits from several lighting types. Evaluate your kitchen's size, shape, ceiling height, available natural light, and materials. Consider how each area functions. Then put layers of lighting to work.

Your choices

ACCENT LIGHTING In the form of track, recessed, or wall-mount fixtures, accent lighting can spotlight architectural elements, collections, or artwork. Low-voltage strips mounted inside glass-front cabinetry help showcase prized dishes or glassware.

AMBIENT OR GENERAL LIGHTING This is the room's basic overall illumination. One or two ceiling-mount fixtures commonly supply ambient lighting, but this can create shadows and cast glare for anyone standing at the room's perimeter. As such, it's best to balance ceiling-mount fixtures with recessed ceiling lights positioned in key areas, such as above work areas.

DECORATIVE LIGHTING While most often used as a design element, this type of lighting also can be functional. Where open kitchens connect to other living areas via steps, for example, strip lights mounted under each riser can provide beauty—and make navigation throughout the area safer.

TASK LIGHTING As the name implies, this type of lighting brightens a specific area or surface where tasks are performed, such as the sink, range, and island. It is achieved with pendants and undercabinet and recessed fixtures, and it eliminates shadows and overhead glare in a specific area, preventing eyestrain.

Bulbology

Most kitchens benefit from a balance of warm and cool tones, which often dictates the fixtures you choose. Each bulb type has pros and cons.

Type	Light	Cost	Use
Incandescent	Warm glow; some tinted to reduce yellow cast; dimmable	Least expensive to buy, but shortest life (least efficient)	Produces heat; best for decorative or mood lighting, or overall illumination
Fluorescent	Diffused, shadowless, may feel cool; color-corrected warm white bulbs create a friendlier mood	Up to 12 times more expensive than incandescent, but last much longer, using one-third of the energy	General illumination
Halogen	Crisp and white, good color rendition	High cost but low voltage, so lasts four times longer and consumes fewer watts than incandescent	Best for task (especially under cabinets) and accent lighting; gives off more heat than incandescent

Glossary

BEAM SPREAD
The area brightened by the light a fixture casts in a room.

CEILING-MOUNT FIXTURE
Provides general illumination from overhead; fixture is installed at the ceiling.

DECORATIVE LIGHTING
The fixture itself is the focus.

LAMP
Another word for bulb.

PENDANT
Hangs from the ceiling via a stem, wire, or cable to provide task and/or general illumination; one fixture may have more than one pendant.

RECESSED FIXTURE
Installs unobtrusively in the ceiling (only its bulb and lens are visible) to provide general and/or task lighting.

TRACK LIGHTING
Ceiling-mount electrified bar that houses movable and directional lights for task or accent purposes.

UNDERCABINET FIXTURE
Compact strip or track that installs under a wall cabinet to provide bright light for a countertop, eliminating shadows. Most use halogen lamps, which show a food's true colors.

resources

appliances

AGA RANGES
877/650-5775
aga-ranges.com

ALL-CLAD METALCRAFTERS
800/255-2523
all-clad.com

AMANA
866/616-2664
amana.com

ASKO
800/898-1879
askousa.com

BLUESTAR
610/376-7479
bluestarcooking.com

BOSCH HOME APPLIANCES
800/921-9622
boschappliances.com

BROAN
800/558-1711
broan.com

CAPITAL COOKING EQUIPMENT
866/402-4600
capital-cooking.com

CUISINART
800/726-0190
cuisinart.com

DACOR
800/793-0093
dacor.com

DCS BY FISHER & PAYKEL
888/936-7872
dcsappliances.com

DELONGHI AMERICA
800/322-3848
delonghiusa.com

ELECTROLUX
877/435-3287
electroluxappliances.com

ELMIRA STOVE WORKS
800/295-8498
elmirastoveworks.com

EVO, INC.
503/626-1802
evo-web.com

FABER USA
508/358-5353
faberonline.com

FAGOR AMERICA
800/207-0806
fagoramerica.com

FISHER & PAYKEL
888/936-7872
fisherpaykel.com

GAGGENAU
877/442-4436
gaggenau-usa.com

GE; GE MONOGRAM
800/626-2005
geappliances.com;
monogram.com

HAMILTON BEACH
800/851-8900
hamiltonbeach.com

HEARTLAND APPLIANCES
877/650-5775
heartlandapp.com

JENN-AIR
800/688-1100
jennair.com

JURA-CAPRESSO
800/767-3554
capresso.com

KENMORE
888/536-6673
kenmore.com

KITCHENAID
Large appliances:
800/422-1230
Small appliances:
800/541-6390
kitchenaid.com

KITCHEN JEWELS
800/444-1963
kitchenjewels.com

LG ELECTRONICS
800/243-0000
us.lge.com

MARVEL INDUSTRIES
800/428-6644
lifeluxurymarvel.com

MAYTAG
800/344-1274
maytag.com

MIELE
800/843-7231
mieleusa.com

PERLICK CORP.
800/558-5592
bringperlickhome.com

SANYO ELECTRIC CO.
800/421-5013
us.sanyo.com

SHARP ELECTRONICS CORP.
866/726-4399
sharpusa.com

SUB-ZERO FREEZER CO.
800/222-7820
subzero.com

THERMADOR
800/656-9226
thermador.com

U-LINE CORP.
800/779-2547
u-line.com

VIKING RANGE
888/845-4641
vikingrange.com

WARING CONSUMER PRODUCTS
800/492-7464
waringproducts.com

WHIRLPOOL CORP.
866/698-2538
whirlpool.com

WOLF APPLIANCE CO.
800/332-9513
wolfappliance.com

ZEPHYR CORP.
888/880-8368
zephyronline.com

cabinetry

ALNO USA
888/896-2566
alnousa.com

AMERICAN WOODMARK
800/677-8182
americanwoodmark.com

**ARISTOKRAFT
CABINETRY**
812/482-2527
aristokraft.com

ARMSTRONG CABINETS
800/527-5903
armstrong.com/cabinets

CABINET WORKS CO.
510/835-2120

DÉCOR CABINETRY
204/822-6151
decorcabinets.com

DIAMOND CABINETS
812/482-2527
diamondcabinets.com

IKEA
United States: 877/345-4532
Canada: 888/932-4532
ikea.com

KLISE MANUFACTURING
616/459-4283
klisemfg.com

KRAFTMAID CABINETRY
800/571-1990
kraftmaid.com

MERILLAT INDUSTRIES
866/850-8557
merillat.com

OMEGA CABINETRY
319/235-5700
omegacabinetry.com

**PLAIN & FANCY
CUSTOM CABINETRY**
800/447 9006
plainfancycabinetry.com

QUALITY CABINETS
972/298-6101
qualitycabinets.com

RICH MAID KABINETRY
800/295-2912
richmaidkabinetry.com

SIEMATIC
siematic.com

ST. CHARLES CABINETRY
662/451-1000
stcharlescabinets.com

TERAGREN
800/929-6333
teragren.com

WELLBORN CABINET
800/336-8040
wellborn.com

**WOOD-MODE FINE
CUSTOM CABINETRY**
877/635-7500
wood-mode.com

countertops

CAESARSTONE
877/978-2789
caesarstoneus.com

CAMBRIA
866/226-2742
cambriausa.com

DALTILE
800/933-8453
daltileproducts.com

DUPONT
800/426-7426
www2.dupont.com

ELKAY MANUFACTURING
630/574 8484
elkayusa.com

EVERLIFE STONE
800/621-8663
everlifestone.com

FORMICA CORP.
800/367-6422
formica.com

**GREEN MOUNTAIN
SOAPSTONE**
802/468-5636
greenmountainsoapstone.com

J. AARON CAST STONE
404/298-4200
jaaroncaststone.com

LG SURFACES
877/853-1805
lghi-macs.com

MEKAL
905/602-6675
mekal.com.br

PROTEAK
866/376-1587
proteak.com

**SILESTONE
BY COSENTINO**
800/291-1311
silestoneusa.com

SONOMA CAST STONE
877/283-2400
sonomastone.com

STARON SURFACES
800/795-7177
staron.com

VETRAZZO LLC
510/234-5550
vetrazzo.co

faucets and fixtures

AMERICAN STANDARD
800/442-1902
americanstandard-us.com

**ARTISAN
MANUFACTURING**
973/286-0080
artisansinks.com

BATES & BATES
800/726-7680
batesandbates.com

BLANCO AMERICA
800/451-5782
blancoamerica.com

BRIZO
877/345-2749
brizo.com

CIFIAL USA
800/528-4904
cifialusa.com

DANZE
877/530-3344
danze.com

DELTA FAUCET
800/345-3358
deltafaucet.com

DORNBRACHT USA
800/774-1181
dornbracht.com/en

ELKAY MANUFACTURING
630/574-8484
elkayusa.com

FRANKE
800/626-5771
frankeconsumerproducts.com

GRAFF FAUCETS
800/954-4723
graff-faucets.com

GROHE AMERICA
630/582-7711
groheamerica.com

HANSA
678/334-2121
hansa.us.com

HANSGROHE
800/334-0455
hansgrohe-usa.com

INSINKERATOR
800/558-5700
insinkerator.com

JACLO
800/852-3906
jaclo.com

JULIEN
800/461-3377
julien.ca

KOHLER
800/456-4537
kohler.com

KWC FAUCETS
678/334-2121
kwc.us.com

LINKASINK
866/395-8377
linkasink.com

MARVEL INDUSTRIES
800/223-3900
lifeluxurymarvel.com

MGS USA
561/218-8798
mgsdesigns.com

MOEN
800/289-6636
moen.com

NATIVE TRAILS
800/786-0862
nativetrails.net

OLIVERI SINKS
800/449-4401
oliverisinks.com/us

PORCHER
800/359-3261
porcher-us.com

PRICE PFISTER
800/732-8238
pricepfister.com

ROHL LLC
800/777-9762
rohlhome.com

SHOWHOUSE BY MOEN
800/289-6636
showhouse.moen.com

STERLING PLUMBING
800/783-7546
sterlingplumbing.com

STONE FOREST
888/682-2987
stoneforest.com

TOTALLY BAMBOO
760/471-6600
totallybamboo.com

**VILLEROY & BOCH
BATH & WELLNESS**
877/505-5350
villeroy-boch.com

WATERSTONE FAUCETS
888/304-0660
waterstoneco.com

lighting

2 THOUSAND DEGREES
847/410-4400
2thousanddegrees.com

ARROYO CRAFTSMAN
626/960-9411
arroyocraftsman.com

EUROLIGHT
416/203-1501
eurolight.com

HUBBARDTON FORGE
802/468-3090
hubbardtonforge.com

KICHLER LIGHTING
866/558-5706
kichler.com

**MEYDA CUSTOM
LIGHTING**
800/222-4009
meyda.com

OMEGA TOO
510/843-3636
omegatoo.com

PROGRESS LIGHTING
864/678-1000
progresslighting.com

REJUVENATION
888/401-1900
rejuvenation.com

SATELLITE
888/401-1900
satellitemodern.com

SEA GULL LIGHTING
800/347-5483
seagulllighting.com

SHADES OF LIGHT
800/262-6612
shadesoflight.com

**THOMASVILLE
LIGHTING**
864/599-6000
thomasvillelighting.com

W.A.C. LIGHTING
800/526-2588
waclighting.com

tile, stone, and flooring

AMTICO INTERNATIONAL
404/267-1900
amtico.com

ANN SACKS
800/278-8453
annsacks.com

ARCHITECTURAL BRICK & TILE
317/842-2888
archbricktile.com

ARMSTRONG
800/233-3823
armstrong.com

ARTISTIC TILE
888/698-8857
artistictile.com

BRUCE
800/233-3823
bruce.com

CROSSVILLE, INC.
800/221-9093
crossvilleinc.com

DALTILE
800/933-8453
daltileproducts.com

MANNINGTON
800/482-0466
mannington.com

PERGO
800/337-3746
pergo.com

SHAW FLOORS
800/441-7429
shawfloors.com

miscellaneous

ACOUSTIC CEILING PRODUCTS
800/434-3750
acpideas.com

ALL-CLAD METALCRAFTERS
800/255-2523
all-clad.com

AMEROCK CORP.
800/435-6959
amerock.com

ATLAS HOMEWARES
800/799-6755
atlashomewares.com

BALLARD DESIGNS
800/536-7551
ballarddesigns.com

BENJAMIN MOORE
888/236-6667
benjaminmoore.com

CHANTAL
800/365-4354
chantal.com

CRATE AND BARREL
800/967-6696
crateandbarrel.com

EMILE HENRY USA
888/346-8853
emilehenryusa.com

FISSLER USA
888/347-7537
fisslerusa.com

GRAHAM & BROWN
800/554-0887
grahambrown.com

HOUSE OF ANTIQUE HARDWARE
888/223-2545
houseofantiquehardware.com

HY-LITE PRODUCTS
800/655-9087
hy-lite.com

IBP GLASS BLOCK
800/932-2263
ibpglassblock.com

IKEA
United States: 877/345-4532
Canada: 888/932-4532
ikea.com

INSINKERATOR
800/558-5700
insinkerator.com

JACLO
800/852-3906
jaclo.com

JOHN BOOS & CO.
888/431-2667
johnboos.com

KLISE MANUFACTURING
616/459-4283
klisemfg.com

KNAPE & VOGT
800/253-1561
knapeandvogt.com

KUHN RIKON
888/662-5001
kuhnrikon.com

LE CREUSET
877/273-8738
lecreuset.com

LIBERTY HARDWARE
800/542-3789
libertyhardware.com

METALLO ARTS
717/739-1088
metalloarts.com

MEYER CORP.
800/214-8369
meyer.com

NOTTING HILL DECORATIVE HARDWARE
262/248-8890
nottinghill-usa.com

PLOW & HEARTH
800/627-1712
plowandhearth.com

POTTERY BARN
888/779-5176
potterybarn.com

PROTEAK
866/376-1587
proteak.com

REV-A-SHELF
800/626-1126
rev-a-shelf.com

SATELLITE
888/401-1900
satellitemodern.com

SUR LA TABLE
800/243-0852
surlatable.com

SHENANDOAH CABINETRY (HARDWARE)
(available at Lowe's)
877/569-3774
shenandoahcabinetry.com

SHOWHOUSE BY MOEN
800/289-6636
showhouse.moen.com

SPECTRA DECOR
800/550-1986
spectradecor.com

STONEWALL KITCHEN
800/826-1752
stonewallkitchen.com

THERMASOL
800/776-0711 (West Coast)
800/631-1601 (East Coast)
thermasol.com